Soft & Cuddly

Soft & Cuddly

Jarett Kobek

Boss Fight Books
Los Angeles, CA
bossfightbooks.com

ISBN 13: 978-1-940535-15-9
First Printing: 2016

Series Editor: Gabe Durham
Book Design by Ken Baumann
Page Design by Christopher Moyer

CONTENTS

ix   Foreword

1   Black Magic on a Cassette Tape

21   The Agonizing Breech Birth of The ZX Spectrum

33   Activate Your Vision

45   To Be an Iron Maiden

63   Give it Back to the Shores of Albion Where the Mills Were First Abused

77   We All Want Our Time in Hell

93   Whatever Happened to the Man of Tomorrow?

101   The Fall of Communism and the Łódź City Coders

113   After Seven Chapters, the Re-Emergence of
              Soft & Cuddly, the Apparent Topic of this Book

119   H.E.X. Magick with the Elemental Woman

125.   I Looked into the Abyss Thinking the Abyss
              Would Look Back Into Me but I Discovered
              That the Abyss is an Asshole Who Won't Make
              Eye Contact

135.   Everything You Ever Wanted is Kept in the
              Refrigerator

143   Time Enough to Sleep, Darlings

157   Epilogue: *Fucker Gamer Scum Get Stabbed*

165   Notes

173   Acknowledgements

FOREWORD

I FIRST DISCOVERED SOFT & CUDDLY after securing a
huge haul of bootlegged ZX Spectrum games from
my friend Thomas. He had refused for weeks to let me
borrow anything from his treasure trove of Spectrum
tapes, insisting that he was playing them all on a daily
basis. Frustrated, I supplied him with several boxes of
the classic C-15 Computape blank cassettes so he could
make me copies of his copies. It took him some time but
he eventually brought them to me on the playground.
I looked at the tapes, scanning over the crudely written
names on the featureless labels and trying to join them
in my mind with the graphics I'd seen in recent issues of
Crash and *Your Sinclair*.

One of the tapes said "soft & cuddly." The title
instantly conjured up images in my mind of a game
called *Ah, Diddums*, a borderline-moronic romp in
which you controlled a teddy bear in a very abstract
room, trying to do god-alone-knows what. Despite

playing it for some time, my sister and I couldn't figure out what the point of it was. So because of *Ah, Diddums, Soft & Cuddly* got pushed aside in favor of better-known titles.

When I finally finished school that day and returned home with my bag of goodies, I set up the ZX Spectrum in the front room, tried to load the first game, and… TAPE LOADING ERROR. It failed. When I think back on this fateful day, most of what I remember is recalled through a sizzling red mist. I went through tape after tape, listening to the broken warble on the header data and watching a pastiche of what should have been the solid blue and red bars blinking onscreen. There must have been around 25 tapes: None of them loaded.

Then I got to the bottom of the bag, and there it was. Shoved aside and passed over for everything that had just failed me. Resentment and resignation mingled with a faint glimmer of hope. I took a sip from my cold cup of tea—I was banned from using the kettle as a result of a previous incident—and put *Soft & Cuddly* into the cassette player. I took the leads in and out: I told myself this made a difference and I still believe it did. I also put my hand on the tape player, as if to reassure it, to try to prepare it to interpret the data correctly rather than producing that familiar, awful warble of failure.

I pressed play.

The signal was strong. The tape sounded as good as an original. The bars onscreen were solid as rock (if the rock was blue and red and projected on a cathode ray tube). I held onto my jubilation, however, as the battle was far from won. Many times in this batch I had encountered tapes that sounded great yet produced the dreaded TAPE LOADING ERROR at the very last moment. I resisted the urge to push down on the lid of the tape caddy, which was sometimes required to load certain games—but to do so mid-load was madness. I was panicking slightly. Could this tape redeem the day? Even if I was to control a moronic teddy bear or some recalcitrant baby and have no clue what was going on, heavens, it would at least be something.

The loading screen appeared. *Soft & Cuddly* written in the top left. A large THE POWER HOUSE logo in the middle. It loaded. The fear of a TAPE LOADING ERROR shattered.

Then an image appeared onscreen, an image that will never leave me: a ghastly, blinking face, framed with what looked like grim pastiches of the Cookie Monster, that appeared to be… eating babies? The face wore a spiked crown—or was it half a mantrap, the other half buried in its scalp? Its lower left eyelid was severed and its frenzied attempts to blink only ever resulted in half of the eye being obscured. What torture had befallen this disembodied head? This was not *Ah, Diddums*. This was nothing like *Ah, Diddums*.

In the days when Mary Whitehouse's idiotic conservatism was rampant and all of the films I wanted to see the most were placed on the VIDEO NASTIES list, could it be that I finally had some form of playable video nasty? Could it be that I could actually cast myself in these fantastically grim environments that my young mind so longed to explore? Would I have to hide this game from my parents?

The game that followed was a desecration of all that I expected of the computer games industry. This was beyond a game. This was a statement, a damning indictment of everything ringfenced and British. It was a pathway from the cosseting, predictable games of that period into something far more abstract and expressive. Something far more individual. Through the conduit of "Soft & Cuddly," we gamers were offered a vision of one man's personal hell.

Many years later I revisited this game for my YouTube channel "Funkyspectrum," where I offer reviews and playthroughs of old Spectrum games, and all of the old feelings I had when I first loaded it up came flooding back. As the many people who have reached out to me about the video would agree, *Soft & Cuddly* has lost none of its bite. It's still shocking. It's still singular. It still stands as a grim beacon, casting its lurid light out across the video gaming landscape. *Soft & Cuddly* remains one of the standout experiences for the ZX Spectrum. As time passes, it seems more at home in the modern world than it ever did in the past. A world that is now, by any stretch of the imagination, anything but soft & cuddly.

George Bum
bumfungames.com
Winter, 2016

1. BLACK MAGIC ON
A CASSETTE TAPE

CONSIDER THE CASE OF JOHN GEORGE JONES. The creative mind behind *Go to Hell* and *Soft & Cuddly*, two games released for the British-made Sinclair ZX Spectrum, a 1982 microcomputer with a whopping 48K of memory.

Go to Hell was published by Activision UK in 1985 under a dummy label called Triple Six. As far as can be determined, it's the very first graphical game that takes place in Hell.

The player explores the infernal netherworld, gathering up a series of multicolored crosses while wandering through a tableau of dancing devils, automated guillotines, and heads bisected by handsaws labeled "DIE."

When the full rainbow of Hell's crosses are collected, the player brings this haul to the giant green face of Alice

Cooper, and, just like in real life, hand-delivering religious icons to a shock-rocker is a kind of beautiful victory.

Soft & Cuddly was published by The Power House, a budget subdivision of the British software firm CRL. It's very reminiscent of *Go to Hell*. The player's mother, the Android Queen, has been dismembered. Her husband, the player's father, has been beheaded.

The player must locate his father—whose body is kept in a refrigerator located at semi-random places across the game's map—and get directions to the parts of his mother's body. Each piece of the Queen must be returned to her husband in the refrigerator. (Every marriage is its own mystery.)

The player explores a grotesque subterranean world, beset on all sides by portly conjoined babies, sheep desecrating gravestones, monsters suffering from undiagnosed eye dystonia, and skulls clad in rakish berets.

•

Sometimes when you're at a party and your brain has turned off its rapid-fire Morse code of suicidal ideation long enough to notice the other striving flesh, you'll see an atheist negging an attractive woman by attacking her belief in astrology. This will often involve trotting out an Arthur C. Clarke quote, which goes: *Any sufficiently advanced implementation of technology is indistinguishable from magic.*

The implication being that when technology advances past a certain point, it appears to transgress the laws of nature and thus, to the uninitiated, becomes a kind of magic. This is why office tech support workers are treated like necromancers. Every society treasures the rare ones who speak big words with the fire.

The Spectrum's ROM came with its own well-regarded implementation of BASIC, but for any high-level programming, a person had to use Assembly. The Spectrum's CPU was the Zilog Z80A, an ultra-primitive microchip best known for powering graphic calculators and teaching Intro Assembly to Comp Sci students.

As far as it goes, Z80 Assembly is not backbreaking. But it is unspeakably annoying, relying on a series of symbols and codes which only increase in complexity when interfaced with the Spectrum's features and quirks.

One of Comp Sci's few truisms is that the first program anyone writes while learning a new language is one that spits out the phrase "Hello World!"

In BASIC, Hello World is simple:

```
10 PRINT "Hello World!"
```

To give a taste of Z80 Assembly's capacity to irritate, here's a variation on a Hello World program, with the greeting replaced by some remarkably obscene Turkish once overheard in the Konak station of the İzmir Metro:

```
org 45000

ld de, jgj
ld bc, $10
call $203C
ret
jgj  defb  "Geber  hain  götcu!
Amına böyle koydum!"¹
```

So picture it. There's John George Jones. He's living in southeastern England. It's the mid-1980s, he's fourteen, and he's programming *Go to Hell* on his ZX Spectrum.

In a few years, he'll be giving batshit interviews and writing astonishing letters to the gaming press. He's using Z80 Assembly, typing in a series of arcane codes and symbols to summon up a tapestry of Hell replete with demons and Satanic doings. It's very possible Alice Cooper is on the stereo.

---

1 The umlauts and dotless 'i' of 'amına' will prevent this program from functioning fully on a Spectrum. Adjust accordingly.

Let's posit a twist on Clarke's idea and suggest that when John George Jones presses the fleshy rubber keyboard of the Spectrum, he is actually, literally, for real, practicing black magic.

Why not?

The symbolism of Z80 Assembly is as dense as the language and ceremonies found in any grimoire. And it's as robust a system of retrieval as any invocation. A person jumps through a series of hoops in the hopes of achieving a predicted result, and if the formula works, then a demonic vision is summoned.

•

The ZX Spectrum was not a home computer of the floppy diskette or the hard drive. The system was older and weirder, part of a generation of microcomputers that used audio cassettes to load and save data.

These cassettes were the same as the ones employed by the recording industry to distribute its wares. Unlike the other discards of the musik bizness, the garden-variety audio cassette has demonstrated a surprising robustness, surviving well past its period of dominance, and entrenching itself as the definitive signifier of 1980s nostalgia. A small number of people use them to the present day.

Imagine being a teenager—and John George Jones was by no means the only one—who had a game professionally published for the ZX Spectrum.

If you held the physical object in your hands, *Soft & Cuddly* was no different than any album by Alice Cooper. It was the same as *Thriller*. The same medium used by pop stars. And you could buy it in the same stores. Sold across the nation.

For that moment, the line between programmer and rockstar ran very, very thin.

•

When *Go to Hell* was released, it didn't transgress past its obvious confines.

It was a cassette bought by people who play games. They liked it or they hated it.

John George Jones was spared all the pleasures of being a modern game creator.

There were no tweets about epic pwnage. There were no articles by freelance journalists about the feels. He didn't watch PewDiePie play his game and wonder when, exactly, the YouTube star had been kicked in the head by a mule. There were no emails from strangers threatening John George Jones with death and informing him that he was a bag of dicks who sucked the shit of God.

All that happened was the appearance of some negative reviews in the UK gaming press.

Do not take this as a reflection of the title's quality. The 1980s were an era of serious payola, with a company's willingness to advertise in a magazine often having a direct relationship to positive reviews.

•

Soft & Cuddly was a different story.

Depending on your perspective, its release in late August of 1987 was either a catastrophe or a masterpiece of timing.

According to Andy Wood, who oversaw sales and marketing efforts for CRL, the parent company of The Power House, financial constraints dictated that review copies be posted via second-class mail on either the 16th or 17th of August. This ensured a delivery of several days' time.

When the games left the office, they were mailed in a novelty of Wood's invention: *Soft & Cuddly* branded airsickness bags. "I had been flying a lot at the time," writes Wood.

Interviewed by *The Games Machine* #2 in December 1987, Ashley Hildebrant, then Managing Director at The Power House, stated that press releases associated with *Soft & Cuddly* arrived on August 20.

As the 20th was a Sunday, Hildebrandt must have been mistaken. Wood suggests that the press packages may have arrived on the 19th.

August 19, 1987 is of significance, as it was a day that played host to one of the most infamous events in recent British history, namely the Hungerford Massacre.

We can easily waste several paragraphs relaying the intimate details of yet another stupid mass shooting perpetrated by yet another useless man. But as these events are now as regular as the phases of the Moon and only grow more depressing, there's no reason to recap the massacre.

Here's a general summary, which you may clip and paste for future use on social media whenever the next senseless tragedy arises: USELESS MAN. GUNS. EXPLOSIONS. DEFENSELESS BODIES. BLOOD. DEATH. CHAOS. POLICE. MORAL OUTRAGE. NORMAL PEOPLE ASKED TO SPEAK IN THE GLARE OF MASS MEDIA ABOUT THE MEANING OF VIOLENCE. POLITICIANS BAPTIZING THEIR CAREERS IN THE SPLATTERED GUTS OF THE INNOCENT. WASH, RINSE, REPEAT.[2]

---

2 If you want something more substantial but in no way more nourishing, find a copy of Jeremy Josephs's book on the subject. It's appeared under two titles. *Hungerford: One Man's Massacre* and *One Bloody Afternoon: The Hungerford Massacre*.

•

Even by the heightened standards of the United States of America, a country given a rare three stars by the Michelin Guide for the quality and flavor of our spree killings, Hungerford was bad. Really bad.

And it happened in a sovereign nation with two distinct attributes: (1) No modern tradition of gun violence. (2) A history of grotesque tabloid reporting.

•

One paper stood out in its coverage. The *Daily Star*—then in a short-lived period of being published as the *Star*—had fixated on a supposed link between the Rambo film *First Blood* and the Hungerford killer.

Several years earlier, the tabloids had convulsed into the Video Nasties scare, a moral panic provoked by the advent of consumer VCRs.

Before the VCR, all cinematic distribution in the UK had fallen under the jurisdiction of the British Film Board, the Home Nations' active censoring body. A loophole allowed films to be distributed on VHS tape without government oversight. Amongst Britain's many hysterics, the thought was that copies of the notoriously shitty *Cannibal Holocaust*—and many other boring films loved by men beclad in black t-shirts and semen-flecked denim—would turn the nation into a slavering mass of rapists and violent criminals.

The tabloid media started calling these films the "Video Nasties."

With no clear origin point, the term would appear to be one of those grotesque misrepresentations that rise up from the fevered imaginations of a thousand journalists. Magical phrases designed to capture, condense, and crush a subject. (How's life after prison, Foxy Knoxy?)

One of the prime shakers and movers of the scare was a former schoolmarm and professional moral scold named Mary Whitehouse. As the head of the National Viewers' and Listeners' Association, she waged a decades-long war that spanned from the early 1960s until the 1990s. Her superpower was the ability to find offensive material in anodyne places.

One of her greatest hits: the 1977 private prosecution of *Gay News* and David Lemon on blasphemy charges for publishing "The Love that Dares to Speak its Name," a poem about Jesus fucking Roman centurions. Whitehouse won at trial. *Gay News* was fined. Lemon received a jail term. On blasphemy charges. In the 20th century.

Another of her victories: neutering *Doctor Who* at its creative peak. She objected to the last shot in episode 3 of 1976's "The Deadly Assassin," in which the Fourth Doctor, Tom Baker, had his head submerged underwater. Whitehouse's belief was that children would not know whether their hero was dead or alive, and thus spend a week trapped in a paralysis of fright and dread. Cowed by the criticism, the BBC fired producer Peter Hinchcliffe, ending the program's first (and only indisputable) Golden Age.

In 1972, Whitehouse took a very public stance against the appearance and promotion of Alice Cooper's "School's Out" on *Top of the Pops*.[3] If the only thing you remember of the song is its chorus, which repeatedly chants the title, then you've pretty much got the whole thing. It's fluffy nonsense about school being out. Nothing more, nothing less.

---

3   Whitehouse offered no objection to Jimmy Savile, the longtime host of *TotP*, who resonated throughout postwar Britain, appearing in the media with the consistency of the North Star. He was a television entertainer who climbed his way into the upper echelons of society, being given control of the country's hospitals (seriously) and serving as a marriage counselor to Prince Charles and Princess Diana. In death, when he couldn't threaten anyone with libel lawsuits, many long-term rumors proved true and Savile was exposed as a serial sexual predator and necrophiliac who robbed bodies of their fake eyes and turned them into rings. In 1977, Whitehouse's National Viewers' and Listeners' Association presented Savile with an award. Presumably for something other than raping the patients of Broadmoor and violating the dead.

Which makes Whitehouse's objection all the more surprising. But then consider her superpower. Offense in anodyne places. Her scolding generated an enormous amount of publicity and helped push "School's Out" to Number One on the pop charts, effectively making Cooper a superstar in the UK.

Her letter to the BBC's head of light entertainment must be quoted:

> I am writing to express the gravest concern over the publicity which has been given Alice Cooper's record 'School's Out'. For weeks now 'Top of the Pops' has given gratuitous publicity to a record which can only be described as anti-law and order. Because of this millions of young people are now imbibing a philosophy of violence and anarchy. This is surely utterly irresponsible in a social climate which grows ever more violent.
>
> It is our view that if there is increasing violence in the schools during the coming term, the BBC will not be able to evade their share of the blame.

It's hard to remember now that Cooper's major cultural footprint is a nationally syndicated radio program that subjects the world to repeated airings of the Blue Öyster Cult's "Nosferatu," but there was a time when

Uncle Alice was the major transgressive figure of the English-speaking world.

Probably the easiest summary, dripping with all of the earnest cluelessness of institutional literature, can be found in an article appearing in *Academic Psychiatry* vol. 27, no. 1 (Spring 2003) entitled "From Alice Cooper to Marilyn Manson: The Significance of Adolescent Antiheroes."[4]

> Alice Cooper emerged in the late 1960s as the band "that drove a stake through the heart of the love generation." Although Alice Cooper was the name of a band, AC was most associated with the lead singer Vincent Furnier… His more parentally distressing songs violated taboos of necrophilia[5] ("I Love the Dead"), violence ("Dead Babies"), and mental illness ("The Ballad of Dwight Fry"). His stage antics were equally provocative, as

---

4 Six (!) authors contributed to this paragraph: (1) Jeff Q. Bostic, MD, Ed.D. (2) Steve Scholzman, M.D. (3) Caroly Pataki, M.D. (4) Carel Ristuccia. (5) Eugene V. Beresin, M.D. (6) Andrés Martin, M.D., M.P.H.

5 "I Love the Dead" appeared on *Billion Dollar Babies*, the 1973 follow-up to *School's Out*. Is it possible that when Cooper visited *Top of the Pops*, he took some tips from ol' Jimmy Savile?

AC dismembered dolls with an axe, assaulted women, and ultimately dramatically acted out a "guillotine" scene of decapitating himself at the end of shows.

Another perspective comes from Sylvain Sylvain, rhythm guitarist for the New York Dolls, in the KISS biography-slash-oral history *KISS: Behind the Mask* by David Leaf and Ken Sharp:

> We were really popular in the Midwest. Back in the very early 70s, if you were a rock band, no matter where you were people came up to you and asked if you were Alice Cooper. They asked you for your Alice Cooper autograph, thinking a band with long hair and looks weird is Alice Cooper.

Every time that Alice Cooper née Vince Furnier trods upon the green grass of Albion, he can't help but tell someone of his pleasure with Whitehouse and her efforts, and how, in his gratitude, he arranged for flowers to be delivered to her home. In some tellings, the flowers are delivered once. In others, they are delivered daily for a span of weeks.

In a way, Whitehouse's efforts set the stage for at least one British lad to imbibe a philosophy of violence and anarchy. In interviews with the present writer, John George Jones has referred to Cooper's influence:

> I was fan of the Alice Cooper group as a kid—quite a rare thing in the synth pop new-romantic 80's in the UK—my favourite album was the much stranger *Pretties For You*. (Still is in fact.)

Go to Hell not only features Cooper's leering 8-bit face, but also takes its title from a song on the album *Alice Cooper Goes to Hell*. *Soft & Cuddly* was originally titled *Love It to Death*, after Cooper's 1971 album.

The Power House asked Jones to change the title.

•

In the days after the massacre, the *Star* hammered on the apparent similarities between *First Blood*—a man in a small town goes on a killing spree—and Hungerford. There was no evidence that the killer had seen *First Blood*, let alone owned a VCR.

In the finest tradition of the tabloid press, this didn't matter.

And then amidst the gore and the spilt ink, there arrived a new video game, packaged in a sick bag, on the desks of news editors across the nation.

In 1987, cassette inlays for The Power House's games had very unique cover art, none of which reflected the content, and all of which were licensed from the painter Tim White.

White produced the kind of oil canvases that graced nearly every volume of *Science Fiction and Fantasy* between 1973 and 1995. The art was hyperrealistic, as precise as Swiss clockwork, and featured all the well-known genre tropes. Robots, aliens, spaceships, ladies of the canyon, creatures with unlikely anatomy. And, as was something of a trademark, a great deal of vegetation.

The Power House repurposed White's old artwork—images previously found on paperbacks—and used them as adornments for their games.

On the cover of *The Bow*, a topless woman is perched in a tree, her crossbow drawn, ready for action. This artwork first appeared on a 1984 French edition of Tanith Lee's *Vazkor, Son of Vazkor*. In the case of *Oddball*, a multi-sided metallic spaceship beams white light down on four solemn pallbearers. This artwork first appeared on the 1979 New English Library edition of Ernest M. Kenyon's *Rogue Golem*. With the game *Swat*, a metallic insect stands perched on a leaf. This artwork first appeared on the 1978 New English Library edition of Terry Pratchett's *The Dark Side of the Sun*.

For *Soft & Cuddly*, The Power House used White's artwork from the 1985 Granada edition of *The H.P. Lovecraft Omnibus 2: Dagon and Other Macabre Tales*.

Ignoring Lovecraft's strategy of keeping unspeakable clenching horrors and eldritch churning blasphemies off the page, White painted a grinning demon perched atop a pile of very realistic severed human heads, each face contorted and bloody, some with eyes open in sightless despair, others with lids closed in blackest death. A tongue juts from one mouth, never again to experience the bioelectric joy of taste. The demon sits like a gargoyle Hamlet, a woman's head in his left hand, her Yorick face mid-scream, forever free of gibes and gambols, gore dripping from the sinus cavity, mouth encircled with sanguinary release.

•

One of the unknowns of *Soft & Cuddly*'s press package is whether or not the material referenced a tagline The Power House had used on the title's promotional posters. These were large-scale reproductions of White's Lovecraft artwork and were distributed with issue #45 (October 1987) of *Crash*, the premier Spectrum periodical.

At the poster's top, in white block letters, were printed the words SOFT & CUDDLY. Immediately below was the tagline, in red letters drawn to resemble dripping blood.

THE FIRST COMPUTER NASTY.[6][7]

•

On August 26, the *Star* ran an article entitled, "New Gory Shocker." Here is a selection:

> The game, called "Soft and Cuddly", goes on sale from Tuesday—just 13 days after the Hungerford killings […] More than 50,000 of the game cassettes, priced £1.99, for the Spectrum computer

---

6 Both Andy Wood and Ashley Hildebrandt have confirmed that the poster, and its tagline, would have predated the Hungerford Massacre. Advertising as prophecy.

7 The threat of the Computer Nasty had hung over the British gaming scene since the fall of 1984, when Parliament passed the Video Recordings Act of 1984. A direct response to the Video Nasties scare, this legislation created a certification for any commercially released VHS product. For a few months, the Advent of the Computer Nasty was discussed in the gaming press, seemingly reinforced by the release of titles like Cosmi's *Forbidden Forest* and Palace Software's very loose adaptation of the Sam Raimi film *The Evil Dead*, which itself was considered one of the worst of the Video Nasties.

will be available for children. [...] Mrs. Mary Whitehouse of the National Viewers' and Listeners' Association said: "This is just crazy. It is the product of a sick society." [...] But [Member of Parliament] for Newbury Michael McNair-Wilson said: "It is up to the Home Secretary to see whether the game is actionable."

It's clear from the text that the article's author did not play the game. The biggest clue is the bald statement that *Soft & Cuddly*'s cover art reflects the gameplay: "And part of it depicts a monster sitting on top of a pile of decapitated heads."

Andy Wood recalls the scandal spreading:

I remember that the phone rang pretty consistently on the following Friday. I was interviewed by Reuters. It was covered on the radio too. Mary Whitehouse also jumped on the bandwagon with some asinine and clichéd quote. I had stressed the point that the 'mother' character in the game (to reassemble) was a robot (cyborg) in case of any comeback, thank goodness. But I could not have anticipated what happened. It was meant to be just some fun 'terrorist punk' marketing. We stood our ground, but the purported and unfounded link to the tragic Hungerford news coverage made me very sad, and devastated for all those involved. […] It was an awful time.

So there was John George Jones, author of *Soft & Cuddly*. Eighteen years old. The teenager who sat at his Spectrum, listened to Alice Cooper, and summoned demons. Denounced by the nation's foremost moral scold, a woman who'd ruined everyone's fun for decades. Condemned by the Member of Parliament whose constituency represented Hungerford.

Now John George Jones was like Alice Cooper. His product in high-street shops, the British equivalent of America's big-box retailers. In the same format as the shock-rocker. Thousands of units across the United Kingdom. Corrupting the youth. Skewered by the national press.

Black magic on a cassette tape.

2. THE AGONIZING BREECH BIRTH OF THE ZX SPECTRUM

IMAGINE A PARALLEL UNIVERSE in which Steve Jobs of Earth-2 had all the same obsessions as Steve Jobs of our own Earth-1: miniaturization, sleek design, typography, the supremacy of advertising, bolstering his public persona through staged events, and a tendency to treat underlings as if they were swollen grapes and he a Sicilian winemaker.

Now imagine a handful of differences: (1) When Steve Jobs of Earth-2 dies, he won't Go to Hell for enslaving the Chinese whilst handing out copies of *Autobiography of a Yogi* and hawking songs off *The Times They are A-Changin'*. (2) Steve Jobs of Earth-2 had a reverse Midas touch. Everything he touched turned, eventually, to shit.

To find this other Steve Jobs, you need not summon up the square planet Htrae. You need only look to Britain in the early 1980s and locate Sir Clive Sinclair, the founder of Sinclair Research Ltd., the company responsible for the ZX Spectrum.

•

The difference between Clive Sinclair and Jobs came down to money. As a born sadist, the latter had an innate understanding of premium branding. Apple was dominated by an idea that inclusion, the bitter fruit of group membership purchased through premium prices, could create an illusion of added value and thus can disconnect price from cost.

Sinclair believed the exact opposite, practicing a Sam Walton theory of retail. Objects sold at low prices in huge volumes, the enormity of the numbers offsetting the low margins. This approach birthed a dubious pattern that would stretch for most of Sinclair's professional life: Establish a release date, find a price point, design around the cheapest available components,[8] and then push the product to market regardless of its readiness.

---

8 If Steve Jobs of Earth-2 does go to Hell, this might be the cause. There were concerns about the sources of Sinclair's components, which tended to come from what *Practical Computing* termed, positively, in its July 1982 issue as, "the sweatshops of component manufacture throughout the world."

From the perspective of the future, this all seems rather quaint. What's worse? Some dodgy components or Foxconn? Steve Jobs 2 might just make it to Heaven.

In the early 1960s, Sinclair founded the eponymous Sinclair Radionics. The company's first products were mail-order electronics kits sold through hobbyist magazines. The kits were followed by hi-fi stereos and other home electronics.

Some of the products worked. Some of the products did not.

Growth was more or less steady until the early 1970s, when the company released the Sinclair Executive, the world's first slimline pocket calculator. It retailed at half the price of the nearest competitor, featured novel engineering, and sported wonderful design.

It made a fortune.

•

As with every fortune, the money brought unexpected consequences. Sinclair Radionics was sent down a cycle of diminishing returns. For whatever reason, the company released one cheap calculator after another, a self-cannibalizing process somehow culminating in a digital watch that literally did not work and destroyed the company's finances.

Without the cash to bring new products to market, Sinclair was forced to accept outside funding via the National Enterprise Board (NEB), a quasi-socialist government initiative established to further industrial development in Britain. As part of the deal, Clive Sinclair was kept on as an idea man and benevolent figurehead but was stripped of his ability to make decisions about the company's future.

And as with any government agency wrestling with technology, the bureaucrats of the NEB dwelt in the realms of the ill-considered and the naïve, believing that the best way to earn back the money they'd sunk into the company was by releasing a barely-functional portable television with a 2″ screen.

The launch failed.

•

Years before he sought funding from NEB, Clive Sinclair had purchased a dummy corporation. This entity was dormant until it became clear that he'd lost control of Radionics. Sinclair changed the dummy corporation's name to Sinclair Instruments Ltd. and then to Science of Cambridge. As he was still at Radionics, the new company was put under the control of an employee named Chris Curry.

Science of Cambridge's first product was a wrist calculator that arrived in an unassembled kit. It's unclear whether the calculator worked, but the company sold 10,000 units.

The profitable launch allowed Curry to field a product pitch from a man named Ian Williamson. The latter had developed a microcomputer out of spare parts, and believed that his design could be sold as a kit for home-assembly. Curry suggested that Williamson work on another design, using specifications that relied on parts used in Radionics calculators. Williamson took up the challenge. He delivered a working model.

At the last minute, Science of Cambridge pulled out of the proposed deal with Williamson. National Semiconductor offered to redesign Williamson's model around their own components, thus significantly reducing the costs of production.

Science of Cambridge entered into a deal with National Semiconductor and brought the latter's revision of Williamson's machine to market. Called the MK14, it sported a stunning 256 bytes of RAM, a 9-digit LED display and a 20-key keyboard.

It sold between 10,000 and 15,000 units.

Science of Cambridge was never intended to be a computer manufacturer, but when the MK14 proved profitable beyond expectations, it became obvious that microcomputers could fund the company.

Work began on what would be called the ZX80.

•

By the time the ZX80 made its way through product development and was ready to ship, Science of Cambridge had undergone changes in management. Chris Curry had departed, going on to found his own very successful microcomputer company.[9] In the summer of 1979, Clive Sinclair assumed full control, having left Radionics with a tin parachute of £10,000.

Certain business practices reasserted themselves. The ultra-low price point, the cheapest components, and, in particular, Sinclair's history as a manufacturer of calculators.

The nexus of all three was in the ZX80's keyboard, a one-piece membrane consisting of 40 pseudo-keys. This made the system an extremely difficult machine on which to type—an issue of some importance, as its ROM came with a custom implementation of BASIC, and much of the system's appeal was in offering a cheap way of "learning computers."

Science of Cambridge implemented a one-touch system, with each key mapped to multiple forms of input.

---

9 Acorn Computers. Best known for getting a contract to produce the BBC Micro as part of the BBC's efforts to improve computer literacy. That Acorn received the contract drove Clive Sinclair to total distraction, a state of affairs reaching its nadir when Sinclair battered Curry with a newspaper in a Cambridge pub called The Baron of Beef. England can be ridiculous.

Depending on the mode, pressing the C key could produce the letter C, the command CLS, or a question mark.

The ZX80 came with 1K of RAM. Its black-and-white RF video interface ran through the CPU, a Zilog Z80A. There was no onboard graphics chip. Each time the system executed an instruction, the screen went blank.

While its immediate predecessor the MK14 could, in theory, be interfaced with cassette recorders for data storage, the ZX80 was the first Sinclair machine to come with an audio in and out designed for this explicit purpose.

The ZX80 was released as a kit for £79.99 in February of 1980. The fully assembled model was available in March for £99.99. It was the first complete microcomputer available for less than £100.

It sold over 100,000 units.

·

With Science of Cambridge renamed yet again, this time as Sinclair Research Ltd., its next system was the ZX81, which launched in March 1981 and was a drastic refinement of its predecessor.

The new model featured a better implementation of BASIC, more RAM, fewer chips on the circuit board, and cheaper prices. £49.95 for the kit, £69.95 for the assembled.

It still had the membrane keyboard. It still had one-touch typing. It still had the black-and-white display. It still used audio cassettes for data storage.

The real innovation was market saturation. Sinclair Research arranged to sell the assembled computer through the high-street bookstore W.H. Smith. If, prior to this, the acquisition of a computer had required knowledge of secret cabals and their obsessions, now any parent could purchase their child a functional micro as easily as buying groceries.

The ZX81 sold over 1,500,000 units.

•

Sinclair's next goal was to make a system that didn't reek of the hobbyist. Fully mainstream. This approach was sound business and bolstered by the company's marketing, which had established the company founder as Uncle Clive, a kindhearted boffin eager to bring innovation to the working classes.

The next model, the ZX82, had a color display. In its more expensive edition, it offered 48K of available RAM, the equal or better of any other microcomputer on the market.

The system came with the trademark Sinclair quirks, again most visible in the keyboard. The membrane was buried beneath a set of Chiclet-sized rubber keys, difficult to type on and unlike any other input in the history of computers.

One-touch typing was taken to absurd extremes. Depending on the mode, pressing the C-key would produce the letter C, the L PRINT command, the CONTINUE command, the PAPER command, or a question mark.

For data storage, the ZX82 again relied on audio cassettes.

The graphics still ran through the CPU, and the new color output came with its own problems. Each 8x8 pixel block supported two colors, designated as paper (background) and ink (foreground). As long as nothing moved, this wasn't much of an issue. But when a moving graphic entered any 8x8 block with its own pre-existing color attributes, the ZX82 reverted all color to the block's information.

In practical terms, this meant that as one played a game and the player's avatar traversed the screen, it often changed colors or was several different colors simultaneously. The effect was equal parts charming and nauseating. (Many games on the system avoided this problem by being mono or duochromatic.)

As a step up from the ZX80 and ZX81, the ZX82 also featured onboard sound. Unfortunately, this came in the form of a small speaker placed beneath the circuit board, only capable of producing 1-bit noises. (What does 1-bit sound like? BLEEP. BLOOP. BUZZ. Repeat until your ears bleed.)

The system's most distinguishing feature was its casing, for which Sinclair's in-house designer Rick Dickinson deserves all the credit. To this day, the ZX82 remains the best-looking computer that the world has seen. It's smaller than a netbook, it's sleek, it's black. Even the rubber keys look great. It arrived in a moment when every other home computer—including the much-vaunted design of the Apple II, its exact shade of chain-smoker beige agonized over by Steve Jobs— looked like crap.

As the ZX82 moved towards market, it assumed its final name.

The ZX Spectrum.

The system was priced at two tiers. £125 for the 16K model. £175 for the 48K.

It had a shit keyboard. It had shit sound. Its graphics bled color. It used audio cassettes to save and load data.

It became the bestselling computer in British history, moving over five million units in its original and subsequent models. It was exported to Spain, where it achieved great success. It was cloned throughout the

Soviet Union and Eastern Europe, selling millions and millions of unlicensed versions.

The Spectrum was a juggernaut.

But before it could achieve any of its success, Sinclair Research would have to perform the biggest miracle of all: Getting out of its own way.

3. ACTIVATE
YOUR VISION

BEFORE *SOFT & CUDDLY,* there was *Go to Hell.*

The first mention of the latter game, anywhere, is in issue #2 (June 1985) of the baroquely-titled *Zzap!64*, a magazine dedicated to the Commodore 64.

Zzap!64 was a fledgling sister publication of *Crash,* which through a mixture of irreverence and enthusiasm had established itself as the preeminent Spectrum gaming magazine. Imagine a professional version of the Steam forums done in print—without the threats of skullfucking—and you'll have the idea.

Two-thirds of the way down issue #2's page 69 is an item entitled, "Enter the video nasties." Accompanying this item is a crude illustration of a zombie's head. The ghastly undead specimen wears a spider as a fashion accessory and juts out its tongue. The zombie's tongue itself is a serpent which itself is jutting out a forked tongue.

The item reads as follows:

I am horrified by whispers reaching my ears from one of the nation's most upright and respectable software houses. Believe it or not they are planning to release a range of scandalous, down market games for demented necrophiliacs[10] starting off with a little number called *Alice Cooper Goes to Hell*. It features screens with heads sawn in half, and people mangled in body crushers. I kid you not.

Naturally the company haven't the courage to release this under their own name, so an evil new label will be established.

Alice Cooper Goes to Hell would see its eventual release as *Go to Hell*, published by a one-off label called Triple Six.

As the article says, Triple Six was a dummy front. The company that released *Go to Hell* was Activision.

The biggest game company in the world.

---

10   While it's impossible to estimate UK necrophiliac population of the 1980s, one suspects that the number was rather low. Which begs the question: If we take this assessment at face value, are we to imagine a boutique label established to serve the microcomputing needs of Jimmy Savile?

In that mid-1980s moment, Activision was nothing like its current incarnation as a faceless behemoth lumbering through the graveyards of the world, desperate to reanimate gaming past with a heady mixture of violence, sex, and human degradation. It had yet to merge with Blizzard.

Back in those innocent days, American software companies were run by suits who still wore suits, MBAs who'd worked their way up the corporate ladder in other industries and then leapt into a new frontier. Few, if any, actually played their companies' products.

They were upright. They were company men. Their eyes were on the bottom line.

By today's standards, gaming was almost unrecognizable, both in its practices and its standards. It was nowhere near the inevitable inflection point that occurs in all arts-based businesses. It had yet to undergo the radical transformation of a hobbyist niche into a full-fledged industry. The people making games were not yet the people who'd spent their childhoods playing video games. No one was native.

Zzap!64's description of Activision as "one of the nation's most upright and respectable software houses" is the crux. Above all else, gaming companies avoided controversy.

The only real counterexample was a small outfit called American Multiple Industries (AMI), which released a handful of titles for the Atari 2600. The most notorious of the lot was *Custer's Revenge*, a game in which the player guides a pixelated General Custer, complete with visible erection, to a mass of pixels described on the game's box as "a ravishing maiden named Revenge." When Custer reaches Revenge—and this is a matter of some dispute—the player either has sex with Revenge or rapes Revenge. (The graphics are so terrible it's impossible to say.) As might be expected, the game generated a furious outcry from the National Organization of Women, Women Against Pornography, Women's Liberation Center of Nassau County, and the American Indian Community House.[11]

Whenever the history of offensive video games is discussed in any depth, *Custer's Revenge* invariably surfaces. It's often the first thing mentioned.

And that's where the counterexample of AMI is of some use. The only reason people remember *Custer's Revenge* is because of its rarity. It was unprecedented.

All of which is to say that *Go to Hell* being published by Activision in 1985 was as likely as ballot initiatives in

---

11 The outcry seems to have been the result of a publicity strategy on the part of AMI. The company invited these groups to screen the game, resulting in a protest, which resulted in news coverage, which resulted in high sales.

California producing good governance, a bright future, and a satisfied citizenry.

Some things are impossible.

Except when they aren't.

•

As the first third-party developer, ever, to provide titles for a console, Activision generated stunning amounts of revenue. The company used 1983 as a year of serious expansion, going public and establishing offices in the UK, France, and Germany.

But the video gods are cruel and wicked and laugh at the plans of mortals. A few weeks following the company's initial public offering, the console market began to collapse. By November of 1983, Activision had laid off a quarter of its workforce.

Annual shareholder reports allow us to gauge the company's financial pain. In the fiscal year of 1983, Activision made $19,200,000 on a net income of $157,600,000. In fiscal year 1986, which saw the release of *Go to Hell*, Activision lost $5,600,000 on a net income of $16,900,000.

Not until 1988 did the company return to profitability.

•

The shareholder report for 1985 makes clear the extent to which the company believed that the video game market was dead. Any future success was in home computers:

> Activision set a number of significant objectives for Fiscal 1985, including executing a transition from primarily a video game developer and marketer to a leading home computer software developer and marketer. [...] The central focus of the report will be the expanding global market for home software and Activision's participation in that global market.

One of the few bright spots is in the report's discussion of the UK market:

> The United Kingdom is currently the most developed (in terms of ownership) home computer market in the world, with one of every five households owning a computer. The UK represents a rare example of hardware homogeneity—over half of its computer households own one type of machine. [...] The United Kingdom also illustrates that a well-established hardware base yields a dynamic software market; the purchase rates of software are higher in the UK than in any other nation. A strong retail base, an active

industry press and vigorous software competition make the UK market and exciting and lively one. […] Activision [has] become the number one software company in Great Britain.

In 1985, as part of its expansion in the home computer market, Activision funded the software development firm Electric Dreams, which was based in Southampton, a city on England's south coast and 125 kilometers from London. Its founder was Rod Cousens CBE. His success with the new company was so complete that in 1989 he was appointed head of Activision International. Electric Dreams disappeared into the bigger company. A stealth takeover by virtue of competence and success.

In an interview for this book, Cousens described the genesis of Activision's international divisions:

Activision was the first multinational company to set up in the UK. […] It had commissioned market research which supported this, it had an experienced management team who had a strong track record in the entertainment industry […] and Activision was taking its lead from that model.

The challenges were in the games and the medium. US-created content was developed on floppy disk due to the success of the Commodore machines whereas Europe was weighted to cassette/tape. This compromised conversion potential and games design, so the idea was to attract dedicated European developers and content. But there was reluctance for it to be published under the Activision brand as there were concerns about quality, etc. Activision actively marketed itself as looking for regional games and developers, and this led to games such as *Go to Hell* coming to the company.

Another of Activision's moves during this period was the acquisition of Infocom. Based in Cambridge, Massachusetts, Infocom's titles included classics like *Leather Goddess of Phobos*, the Zork series, and an adaptation of *The Hitchhiker's Guide to the Galaxy*. Its reputation, bolstered by its proximity to the Massachusetts Institute of Technology and the amount of care and design put into its packaging, was stellar. Infocom was the place where smart people made smart games for smart players.

Its titles were text-based, operating on a call-and-response catechism. Users were plopped into a scenario and given a description of a room: *YOU ARE STANDING IN OVAL OFFICE OF THE WHITE HOUSE. THE PRESIDENT IS SMILING AT YOU. THERE IS A DOG*

HERE. THE DOG IS ADDICTED TO PAINKILLERS. THE PRESIDENT IS ITS PUSHER.

The game then prompted the user for input. The user typed in commands, hoping that they'd discerned the appropriate noun-and-verb combination. Most of the time, the user failed. The games responded with text like: *I'M SORRY, I DON'T UNDERSTAND.* Or: *I DO NOT KNOW THE WORD "PAINFUL DEATH UNTO ANY MAN WHO SHAVES THE HEAD OF MICHEL FOUCAULT."* [12]

Activision merged with Infocom in 1986. The gold standard of video gaming was forging a future with the standard bearers of computer gaming. [13]

---

12 Most people, when referring to the genre, used the terms "text adventures" or "adventure games," but Infocom had been birthed at MIT, one of the epicenters of globalized warfare and its attendant newspeak. The company coined the term "Interactive Fiction." True to form for geek culture, this neologism manages somehow to degrade both interactivity and fiction.

13 The merger's come down through history as a disaster for Infocom, with the Cambridge company being a beautiful flower crushed in an ogre's caress of market-shares and capitalism. This fairy tale's problem is that by the time Activision pulled the plug on Infocom in 1989, there were probably fewer than 5,000 people still willing to pay money to type KICK DOG into their computer and be bombarded with twee narration.

In the annual shareholder report for Activision's fiscal year 1987, amongst its crowing about the merger, there is a notable sentence: "Starting with *The Lurking Horror*, the first computer horror game, Infocom will continue in its tradition of originality in the realm of interactive fiction."

Even on the surface, the validity of this claim—the first computer horror game—is false. It's true that horror games in the early-to-mid 1980s had nothing like their present prominence. But several preceded *The Lurking Horror*. The arguable first, arriving in 1984, was Palace Software's adaptation of *The Evil Dead*.

•

Whilst investigating *Go to Hell*, the author contacted the following former employees of Activision's London office: the aforementioned Rod Cousens, Geoff Heath OBE, Peter Bilotta, Hilary Sable, Anthony Baring, Roger Large, Hugh Rees-Parnall, Allison Hale, Graeme Devine, and Andrew Wright. This represents the lion's share of people who worked at Activision UK in 1984 and 1985.

Beyond a handful of gossamer-thin memories about the title and its possible sales, none of these people could recollect anything about *Go to Hell*. No one remembers who brought the game into the company. No one remembers anything about its development.

It's like a ghost, dimly seen and hardly recognized.

•

Since 1934, the Security Exchange Commission, the governing regulatory body over publicly traded US corporations like Activision, has had Rule 10b-5, which actively prohibits "any untrue statement of a material fact." Basically, Rule 10b-5 means that publicly traded companies aren't allowed to lie in public, particularly about anything with profit potential.

Given the way that Activision was hyping the acquisition of Infocom and its titles in the shareholder report, any statement about *The Lurking Horror* was material fact. Yet an untrue statement is made. *The Lurking Fear* is called the first horror game for the personal computer.

This error is particularly strange, as Activision itself had already published a horror game for the personal computer.

Go to Hell.

Whatever else, this isn't a book written by a total paranoid. No one is arguing that Activision offered a deliberate falsehood. There's no reason why they would.

Far more likely is that *Go to Hell* was lost in the shuffle of a company going through extreme financial distress and upheaval. If no one in the UK has any idea who was responsible for the title, then why would people in the US?

We enter the realm of extreme speculation, but it doesn't seem impossible that no one in California even knew that the game existed.

•

Someone at Activision UK—and we still don't know who—decided to publish *Go to Hell* at the most desperate moment in the company's history. There was also some recognition, be it driven by marketing or concerns about tarnishing the company, that something as scandalous as *Go to Hell* could not be published directly.

A dummy label is set up. A fake. It's given the name Triple Six. Efforts are made to disguise its relationship to the parent company. A ghost floats out into the world.

A game that no one remembers published by a company that doesn't exist.

4. TO BE AN
IRON MAIDEN

THE SPECTRUM WAS ANNOUNCED at the end of April 1982, during the first month of the Falklands War.

To understand the Falklands, you have to wrestle with the best-kept secret of the 20th century: England lost the Second World War. Or perhaps it's more charitable if we paraphrase J.G. Ballard and say that the British won on a technicality.

The capital city was cratered with bomb sites, half a million people were dead, the population was on rations until 1954, and, most significant of all, the war dealt the Empire a mortal blow.

India and Pakistan gained their independence in 1947, stripping away the economic engine that had powered the machine, presaging the slow loss of all the crown's jewels.

The real humiliation came with the 1956 Suez Crisis, during which the British (along with the French and the Israelis) invaded Egypt and then were forced to retreat by an unlikely international coalition headed by the USSR and the United States.

Before World War I, the British Empire was the most powerful force in history. Now it took orders from upstarts. The old boss meeting his replacements.

By the mid-1960s, Britain had metamorphosed from an empire on which the sun never set to a pisshole island in the North Atlantic. Whatever influence the British could exert over world affairs—and it was very little—came through attempts to talk sense into Americans with outré names like James Jesus Angleton.

The early-to-mid period novels of John le Carré are a meditation on this collapse. *Tinker, Tailor, Soldier, Spy* is about a mole used to misdirect the British not because the Russians believe that the British in-and-of themselves possess any specific value, but because the British are a conduit to Washington. The entirety of the state viewed as nothing more than a gateway drug to the real stuff, the source, the actual power.

From the greatest power on Planet Earth to doormen for Our American Cousin.

•

After 1945 came the Postwar Consensus, an unspoken general agreement amongst the British people and the ruling class. The war had wreaked carnage on all levels of society, and that sacrifice would be honored by the creation of a quasi-socialist state and a redefinition of the relationship between the government and its people.

The greatest achievement of this period was the National Health Service, which guaranteed cradle-to-the-grave health care. It was a radical step for a nation that had, less than fifty years earlier, allowed London's East End to fester with miasma and disease.

By the mid-1970s, the Consensus had grown fragile. Briefly: The economic models used since the end of World War II—Keynesian approaches centered on high government spending—stopped working after the United States pulled out of the monetary gold standard and sparked the Oil Crisis, which in turn kickstarted a global recession characterized by incredible inflation and stagnant growth in Western countries.

In response, the UK government, under both the Conservative party of Prime Minister Edward Heath and the post-1974 Labour government, doubled down on the Keynesian economics. Things got so bad that the United Kingdom was forced to take a loan from the International Monetary Fund—the exact sign of a country gone to total shit.

The chaos reached a crescendo with the winter of 1979, which was marked by the inability of a Labour government to deal with violence, strikes, rising piles of trash, and bodies in a Liverpool warehouse.

Everything was fucked.

And then came Margaret Thatcher.

•

She was the Iron Lady. A grocer's daughter who worked her way to the head of the Conservative Party and managed to install herself as Prime Minister in 1979,[14] staying in that office for nearly twelve years. The first female PM in British history and the longest-serving, of any sex or gender, in the 20th century.

A distillation of her political philosophy: Greed, in all of its base forms, is good, and any government's sole function is to encourage greed at the highest and most organized levels. This meant the lowering of taxes on the richest whilst attacking social(ist) services.

---

14 The Tories only won 43% of the vote in the election that brought Thatcher to 10 Downing, but Parliamentary democracy is a bit shit. The same thing happened again—to an even worse extent—in 2015, with the Conservatives winning a working majority with only 37% of the vote. And this says nothing of Stephen Harper's dark reign in Canada, or recent election results in Denmark. It's enough to make an American wonder if maybe the two-party system is a good thing after all. (Just kidding. Donald Trump.)

The philosophy stuck. Its greatest adherent was Tony Blair, who believed in everything that Baroness Thatcher had preached but had learned from her mistakes. Blair arrived in 1997, toothy smile like Violator from Todd McFarlane's *Spawn*, and did the Bill Clinton: disguising globalized deregulation beneath finger-wagging and a shower of Leftist truisms.

The consequences of Thatcher's reign are now fully visible. London has become the world's number one destination for laundering blood money. A city where real estate, Warhols, and Tamil sex-slaves are traded like candy and paid for with the proceeds of Oil Feudalism. It's a sewer of a place, the evilest spot on earth.

•

But none of this quite gets at the nature of Thatcher, or what she really represented, or why any of it matters in the context of a book about a game featuring beret-wearing skulls.

In his elaborate *Tardis Eruditorum*, a serial-by-serial commentary on *Doctor Who*, Philip Sandifer penned an essay with the title "Pop Between Realities, Home in Time For Tea 23 (The Winter of Discontent)." It's of particular interest because it's where Sandifer offers the best explanation yet of Thatcher's importance beyond the simple push-and-pull of ugly politics.

Sandifer suggests that the underlying ideas of the Post-War counterculture, of Leftism and theoretical academics were built on the simple fallacy that even if the individual battles were being lost, the overall campaign towards progress would be won, and that victory would be achieved through an embrace of virtues inaccessible to the enemy.

There was a myth that postmodernism, itself inherently reliant on techniques developed in the avant-garde, could not be adopted, corrupted, or misused for purposes outside of its presumed native territories. There was a secret language spoken by the young and the radical, a hidden alphabet one could read only after one had brute-forced their way to enlightenment through the purchase of the Beatles' *White Album* and books by Guy Debord.

The assumption was that the old order was incapable of learning the new talk, that the nobility of those on the Right Side of Things prevented their approaches from being copied for ill purposes.

Thatcher was the first politician to demolish this assumption. Every aspect was stage-managed not towards sincerity or competence but towards the illusion of sincerity and competence. She understood, in her bones, that what appeared in the news was a shadow bearing only the slightest resemblance to what happened in the corridors of power, and that as a result, any politician worth their salt need not worry themselves about conveying anything about the way that government, and society, actually worked.

One needed only to manipulate the shadow. Very, very few people cared about the rest. And those who did make noises tended to be pinkboys who still believed in Marxism.

Her rise is the moment that defines the ensuing decades. It's the beginning of year after year after year of politics and entertainment conflating, and year after year of a complete fog amongst the governed about what their governments are doing.

If you ever wonder why what you encounter in the free media has as much truth as a *Pravda* editorial, then Thatcher is the answer.

And if you ever wonder how she did it, then it's another simple answer.

Thatcher looked at the Left—at all the wacky idiots who had immersed themselves in a rhetoric and praxis around the impossibility of truth and used these tools to stage puppet shows at anti-war demonstrations—and she applied their techniques to a higher form of untruth.

Postmodern governance.

•

Her first few years in office—particularly the *annus horribilis* of 1980—did not stop the social disarray that had brought her into power. Inflation remained out of control. Race relations sank to all-time lows. There were riots in the streets. At the beginning of 1982, the polling indicated that Mrs. Thatcher's government was careening towards defeat in the next general election.

And then Argentina invaded the Falklands.

•

The Falklands, or the Malvinas, are an archipelago about 300 miles east of Patagonia, the sovereignty of which has been in dispute since the eighteenth century. They were, and are, one of the last few outposts of the British Empire.

Faced with economic crisis at home, the ruling military junta in Argentina convinced itself that an invasion would be easy and bloodless, as surely the British wouldn't defend islands thousands of miles from home. The belief was Argentina's military success would distract its population from the many economic crises of the moment.

As with most proposed bloodless military victories, the end result was rather different. The UK responded in full force and kicked the living fucking shit out of the islands' invading forces.

·

All the while, back in Britain, Sinclair Research was bungling the ZX Spectrum.

The April 1982 launch had gone off gangbusters. The Spectrum debuted on April 23 at a press conference held at London's Churchill Hotel, and the system was on display throughout the weekend at the Earls Court Computer Fair.

The response of the computer press was uniformly positive. The stage was set for Sinclair's triumph in the mainstream.

The only problem? The ZX Spectrum wasn't ready.

·

To gauge the early months' clusterfuck, we need only scan the issues of *Popular Computing Weekly* that appeared throughout the spring, summer, and fall of 1982.

In its May 6 issue, the magazine featured a very positive review and favorable coverage of the just-announced Spectrum.

In the June 10 issue, it ran an editorial that read:

When Clive Sinclair launched the Spectrum, he said, "Delivery within 28 days."

That was seven weeks ago.

Every day that passes more people who were counting the days to the arrival of their new computer call us up asking for help.

There is only so much we can do. We can mention that the promised delivery dates of the Spectrum seemed to have slipped.

More normally we are always willing to take up individual complaints from customers against suppliers.

But when it comes to such a rush of complaints the responsibility necessarily has to fall back in the hands of you, the customer.

The answer is to add a clause to your order stating: "I regard it as binding that the goods are delivered within 28 days."

If your order and cheque are accepted so is the contract.

If your goods are not delivered, go to your Citizens' Advice Bureau, ask about the Small Claims Court procedure, and make a fuss.

The June 16 issue contains a news item with the headline: DESIGN FLAW HALTS SPECTRUM DELIVERY.

The June 24 issue contains a news item with the headline: ZX82 BACK IN FULL PRODUCTION.

The July 1 issue contains a news item with the headline: SPECTRUM GET TO THE CUSTOMER. Its first paragraph reads: "Delivery of the first production run Spectrums has now taken place."

The July 15 issue contains a news item that suggests that the previous article was premature. The headline: LONG WAIT STILL FOR SPECTRUM. Its final paragraph reads: "It seems likely that buyers will have to wait until at least the end of August before the hoped for 28-day delivery is achieved."

The August 5 issue contains a letter from reader Michael Diamond of Glasgow, which has been titled, "Hey! Where's ma Spectrum?" Its first paragraph reads: "It is nine weeks since I sent off my order for a Sinclair ZX Spectrum. It is seven weeks since my cheque was cashed."

The August 19 issue contains an item with the headline: SPECTRUM DELAY PROMPTS GIFT ORDER. It is quoted below:

Those waiting for a ZX Spectrum can expect to have to wait at least 12 weeks before delivery of their orders.

This is the situation described in an open letter released by Clive Sinclair.

He explains that the problems have been due to initial production delays and orders far exceeding expectations.

Production of the machines is now apparently running smoothly at 5,000 units per week and should rise over the coming months. The letter continues, "We are confident that our order backlog will be cleared by September."

The October 7 issue contained a news item with the headline: SPECTRUM PLUGS IN NEW SOCKETS. The relevant sentence: "In order to solve some of the production difficulties which have plagued the Sinclair machine since its launch, the main printed-circuit board has now been redesigned."

With the December 16 issue, the saga came to its end: SPECTRUM GOES ON SALE AT W.H. SMITH.

•

If the Argentine junta's goal was to distract a populace from economic problems and rejuvenate a national spirit of warmongering, then they succeeded beyond belief. The only problem was that their ruse worked in the wrong country.

The Falklands War was the moment of final connection between the Iron Lady's media savvy and wide swaths of the UK public's desire to be manipulated. A renewed jingoism infected the English, cheered on in the red top tabloids. One infamous headline ran in the *Sun*, on the sinking of the Argentine warship the ARA General Belgrano: *Gotcha!* The subheadline read: *Our lads sink gunboat and hole cruiser.*

In June of 1982, Argentina conceded defeat. Control of the Falklands was returned to the British. The Iron Lady was firmly entrenched. The Conservatives maintained control of 10 Downing Street until 1997. Mrs. Thatcher's agenda could be furthered with great impunity.

Her eyes fell on Sinclair Research and the ZX Spectrum.

•

Back in the late 1970s, when the NEB took control of Sinclair Radionics, they discovered that the company had been making £1,000 donations, yearly, to the Conservative Party. It's impossible to say whether or not this is how Sinclair first appeared on Thatcher's radar. It couldn't have hurt.

The more likely explanation is that Mrs. Thatcher or her advisers simply read the newspapers. Through sales and publicity, Clive Sinclair had become the public face of British computing. The story of Sinclair Research (the quasi-socialist bailout of Radionics ignored like bad gas at a white-tie event) was very much a myth that bolstered Thatcher's agenda of British free market entrepreneurialism. And there was nothing that Mrs. Thatcher liked so much as a media myth.

From the perspective of the future, where every six months President Obama hosts a roundtable with Mark Zuckerberg and Elon Musk to discuss how STEM reform can lead to an American military powerhouse that will transform illiterate Middle Eastern peasants into shattered pieces of illiterate meat for decades to come, there's nothing novel about a politician embracing computers.

But credit where it's due. With her science degree from Oxford's Somerville College, Thatcher was the first world leader to understand the financial benefits of a nation with computers in every home. Or the illusion of those benefits.

The Spectrum was a perfect totem of the moment. It was a computer that existed, primarily, in the imagination of its creators. Nothing is as postmodern as a device that harvests money but which no one can use.

•

In the early summer of 1982, while his company was cashing cheques for computers it could not deliver, Clive Sinclair met with the Prime Minister.

The meeting must have gone well. On July 12, Thatcher announced a £9M scheme to install computers into every primary school in the country, in which the Department of Industry would match local funds 50/50. Three systems were considered appropriate for educational purposes. Amongst them was the ZX Spectrum, a system that Sinclair could not ship.

In September, Mrs. Thatcher traveled to Japan and presented Japanese Prime Minister Zenko Suzuki with a Spectrum, intoning in the archest of voices, punctuated by aeon-long pauses, "Prime Minister, this is… a… small… home… computer…"[15]

Time has made this image quaint. Retro-kitsch of the early digital era. In the moment it was something else. A shot over the bow, a way of saying that the United Kingdom could beat the Japanese at their own game. Britain was back. Clive Sinclair was leading the way.

---

15 A letter in the October 21 edition of *Popular Computing Weekly* comments on Mrs. Thatcher's gift: "I was watching ITV news bulletin on September 21 when on came an item about the Prime Minister's visit to Japan. It stated that Mrs. Thatcher awarded the Japanese Premiere an English built computer, a Sinclair Spectrum. I would like to know when Mrs. Thatcher ordered her Spectrum and how long it took her to get it, because I have been waiting 18 weeks for mine." (Sinclair Research custom-built three Spectrums for the event.)

On December 8, 1982, in a speech opening the Information Technology Conference at the Barbican, Mrs. Thatcher elaborated:

> The first ingredient of our approach is a passion-ate belief in the virtues of free enterprise and individual endeavour... Many of the greatest innovations and applications have stemmed from personal initiative. The development of the cheap home micro-computer is an outstanding exam-ple today. I was pleased during my recent visit to Japan to be able to present to the Japanese Prime Minister, in the very temple of high technology, a Sinclair Home computer conceived, designed, and produced in this country. Out into the mar-ket, ahead of its Japanese rival.

Imbued with the social sanction of Britain's most powerful politician, Sinclair Research and the ZX Spectrum entered 1983. It would prove to be a year of astonishing highs.

In 1982, Sinclair controlled over 50% of the UK microcomputer market, selling almost 300,000 units of its various models. By February of 1983, Sinclair had sold over 200,000 Spectrums, and the machine was available in all the best high-street retailers: W.H. Smith, Boots, Currys, Greens, and John Menzies. Around

Easter, Sinclair was moving 40,000 units a month. Sales were in the tens of millions of pounds.

On June 11, 1983, exactly a year and a day after *Popular Computer Weekly* had published an editorial denouncing Sinclair Research's inability to deliver on its promise of 28 days' delivery, Clive Sinclair was knighted as part of the Queen's Birthday Honours. His name had been put forward by Margaret Thatcher herself.[16]

---

16 1983 was the first year that Mrs. Thatcher put forward another name for knighthood. None other than Jimmy Savile, the infamous necrophiliac and serial rapist of the mentally ill. The request was denied by that year's Honours Committee. Mrs. Thatcher would forward Savile's candidacy each subsequent year and have it denied until, in 1990, Jim at last received his Knighthood. How's about that, then?

5. GIVE IT BACK TO THE SHORES OF ALBION WHERE THE MILLS WERE FIRST ABUSED

THE ZX SPECTRUM WAS NOT JUST A BID to reassert the relevance of British manufacturing. It was also a bit of a scam on the working classes. Just read what Mrs. Thatcher said in a speech on March 26, 1983, to the Conservative Central Council:

> Think of the successful new businesses which did not exist ten years ago and were not dreamt of twenty years ago. Think of Clive Sinclair and his microcomputers—virtually every secondary school in the country now has a microcomputer as a result of this Conservative Government's programme.

> And that created a lot of business too. For the parents feel they have to buy computers to keep up!

For the parents feel they have to buy computers to keep up!

Is there any reading of this as something other than an admission that Thatcher's public championing of the microcomputer was a strategy to create parental anxiety for the benefit of British manufacturing?

•

Some computers were more of a scam than others. The moneyed didn't have to buy cut-rate systems with color bleed, fake keyboards and 1-bit sound. They could purchase a BBC Micro or an Amstrad CPC or, more rarely, an Apple II.

All were easier to use than the Spectrum. That's the scam. A system unleashed as a cheap way to learn new technology and keep our Peter well-versed in computers or summat was, by virtue of its quirky engineering, a very difficult teaching tool.

•

But tens of thousands, and then hundreds of thousands, and then millions of Spectrums were floating around the British Isles. They were mostly in the hands of kids.

So what were those kids going to do with their computers?

It might've been hard to program the Spectrum, but it was easy enough to run software. All you needed to do was type LOAD (by pressing the J key) and a set of quotation marks, hit enter, and press play on one's cassette deck. The software could take upwards of ten minutes to load—and there was always the threat that the process could crash with the infamous "R Tape loading error, 0:1" message—but once the code was in memory, you were ready to go.

The Spectrum did not multitask. There was no on-system storage beyond its 48K of memory. It ran a single program at a time. Nothing more, nothing less. When you rebooted, the program disappeared from the system's memory, gone until you loaded it again from cassette.

The keyboard made the Spectrum useless for business and productivity software. But games didn't cost much, with an average price around £7 (about £16 in today's money) and almost never going above £9.95. Budget titles retailed at £1.95.

As Sinclair Research had convinced so many retailers to stock the system, these outlets also carried software. A vast distribution network was in place.

Hard numbers best speak of the Spectrum's reach. Excluding any utilities or applications, the archive on World of Spectrum, the system's definitive internet resource, lists 10,724 games. Almost all of them were coded and published in Britain.

By comparison, GameFAQs.com lists 1,573 games for the Nintendo Entertainment System.

•

The NES was a closed system. The vast majority of people who played games on Nintendo's console could not create or release their own software. It wasn't just unimaginable, it was literally impossible. The flow of information ran one way.

The Spectrum was open. Its method of data distribution was the humble audio cassette, and blank tapes could be purchased anywhere.[17] Anyone who suffered to learn the Spectrum's quirks could produce a game. Anyone could sell them.

But who were the people writing software for the Spectrum?

They were young and they were boys. Besides their youth and overwhelming maleness, they were not

---

17 Purists will no doubt mention the ZX Microdrive, an alternate method of magnetic tape data storage engineered by Sinclair Research. While Microdrive cartridges existed, and were used in game development, they were costly, unreliable, and never really caught on.

emerging from the upper classes. There were no queues of Etonians or King's Scholars offering their services to the software houses of Manchester and Liverpool.

If we take as assumed an idea from the previous chapter—that Margaret Thatcher embraced the Spectrum not because of the system's inherent value but because the Spectrum was a useful tool at a certain moment—then we should acknowledge that, in an accidental way, the Iron Lady ended up being right.

If you're at all skeptical about the influence of computers and information technology on society—and if you aren't then something is terribly wrong with you—then some of your skepticism must be complicated by the hobbyist era.

Whatever the purpose of Thatcher's rhetoric, there's something powerful about a cheap British-made system being programmed by people otherwise excluded from any say in British life.

•

In 2014, Steven Howlett self-published a memoir of his time as a schoolyard Sinclair aficionado. Entitled *Diary of an 80s Computer Geek*, the book is a study in how a bright kid in the Thatcher years could become both an author and publisher of software.

Howlett tells the story of creating his first game, *Ticking Bomb*, in Sinclair BASIC for the ZX81, and selling it for £25 to a computer magazine that published the source code within its pages. The process was repeated with a second game, *Desert Tank*.

After months' more work, Howlett finished another game. This one was for the ZX Spectrum and called *Break Point*, which was a billiards-themed quiz game. Howlett started his own mail-order business. He bought a small advertisement in *Crash*. The gambit was unsuccessful. Six orders came in.

Howlett decided to approach software companies. He sent *Break Point* to ten different firms. He received nine rejections and one acceptance. The latter came from Top Ten Games, who changed the game's name to *Snookered*.

Time passed. Top Ten failed to send royalty payments. Howlett discovered that he couldn't find a copy of his contract. The software company refused to supply a new copy and instead offered him £200. He consulted a lawyer, who told him that without much evidence, there was no real way forward. He took the £200.

In the meantime, *Crash* had begun including cassettes glued to the cover of the magazine, essentially selling software in the hopes of boosting circulation. Using the original title of *Break Point*, Howlett sent *Snookered* to the magazine. *Crash* published the game as a cover tape. They paid him £250. Howlett had gambled, successfully, that Top Ten Games wouldn't sue, as any lawsuit suit would've required the company to produce his contract.

Howlett submitted another game to *Crash*. This one was called *Ultimate Warrior*.[18] Instead of taking another £250, Howlett asked *Crash* to give him half a page to advertise his own mail-order business. *Crash* agreed. On *Ultimate Warrior*'s loading screen, he included another advertisement for his business. The orders flooded in. The next several weeks of his life were dominated by duplicating and mailing tapes.

Crash asked for another game. Sensing that the 8-bit market was falling apart, Howlett declined the offer. He never returned to software production.

•

And then there was the Superstar.

The two most famous Spectrum games, *Manic Miner* and its sequel *Jet Set Willy*, were authored by a teenager from Merseyside named Matthew Smith. *Manic Miner*

---

18   Howlett's memoir plays a bit loose with *Ultimate Warrior*, implying that it was programmed from scratch. In fact, the game was constructed using *3D Game Maker*, an out-of-the-box kit for isometric games. *3D Game Maker* was released in 1987 by CRL, the same publisher that owned The Power House.

was the first Spectrum title to have continuous in-game sound, a feat previously considered impossible.

Jet Set Willy, in which the titular character explores a house bought with the proceeds from his exploits in *Manic Miner*, was hugely influential. Sometimes in big details, like inspiring a flood of platformers for the Spectrum in which an avatar navigates a contained space whilst beset by odd creatures. Sometimes in the small. Miner Willy wears a bowler hat in *Jet Set Willy*, a sign of his new wealth. Cue the digital hatter's dream: years and years of Spectrum avatars sporting headwear from the 1950s.[19]

If you watch any interview done with Smith over the last fifteen years, it's hard to avoid feeling that the Spectrum ruined his life.

He was a teenager who programmed at night on a TRS-80 in his mother's house.[20] He ended up selling at least a million copies of *Jet Set Willy*. He made a minor

---

19 John George Jones's *Soft & Cuddly* would emulate both aspects, its avatar exploring an entire landscape reminiscent of "The Chapel" in *Jet Set Willy* while wearing a bowler hat.

20 Smith programmed at night because his many hardware modifications caused the TRS-80 to crash whenever someone put on a kettle. One of the mods he'd built for the machine was an interface between it and his Spectrum. This allowed him to code and compile on the former and dump to the latter in two seconds' time, thereby routing around the Spectrum's many annoyances.

fortune. He became something of a celebrity, receiving national coverage in the news media. All before he turned twenty years old.

He then abandoned game development and ended up living in a Dutch commune. He was deported by the Netherlands. He disappeared for years, a situation that caused much internet speculation and granted him an almost mythological status. People traded stories on websites dedicated to his whereabouts. Some boasted of knowing his sister. Others said he was right dead, mate. He finally resurfaced in the early-2000s and now, with all the money gone, lives with his mother in the home where he created *Manic Miner*. He's back to programming in the room where it all started.

•

There are others.

People like Mark Butler, Eugene Davis, and David Lawson. Like Matt Smith, they were all from Merseyside, and again like Smith, all three had worked for Bug-Byte, a software house in Liverpool.

When the trio quit Bug-Byte, they formed Imagine Software to make games for the then-new Spectrum. Their first game was the *Space Invaders* clone *Arcadia*. It came out in time for the 1982 Christmas season. As there were almost no titles then available for the

Spectrum, *Arcadia* sold in ridiculous quantities. Some reports suggest over a million units in total sales.

The young men earned more money than they could comprehend. Their company moved from a single room to a gigantic office with more than 70 employees.

They wasted cash on the requisite nouveau-riche accoutrements. Cars, clothes, flesh, motorcycles. Flash, bling, flash, bling. Like a strobe of scintillating scotoma presaging the arrival of terrible business decisions.

Within a year and a half, Imagine Software crashed and burned.

The story itself is not remarkable. It's a repeating pattern. What makes Imagine special was that the company allowed filmmakers to document the unraveling for an episode of the BBC2 series *Commercial Breaks*.

The spectacle played out with the minute imagery of unforgettable television: A cassette duplicator demands a £50,000 cheque and is kept waiting in the lobby. Imagine's financial director bullshits on the phone, trying to raise money, his face falling as he realizes that there will be no more. In the money shot, the staff comes back from lunch and finds they've been locked out of the offices by the bailiff's agents. End of tape.

•

And then there's John George Jones.

He received a Spectrum in 1982, when he was thirteen years old. He remembers being disappointed because Sinclair BASIC was so slow. A friend up the road taught him to program in machine code.

Machine code. Not Assembly. He says that he made his first short programs by converting handwritten designs in mnemonics and then translated this into data that was directly poked into memory. At the time, there was no Assembler for the Spectrum.

What's the difference?

Imagine that you want to eat spaghetti with tomato sauce. If you live in a world where there's an Assembler, you can go to the store, buy the pre-made pasta and buy the pre-made tomato sauce. You take your purchases home and put them together. It takes time and patience and some skill.

In a word without an Assembler, you have to grow the tomatoes and the wheat. You have to wait for the tomatoes to ripen. You have to separate the wheat from its chaff with a flail. You have to hand-grind the wheat into flour. You have to make your own dough. You have to run the dough through a spaghetti mold. You have to cut the dough to the appropriate length. You have to cut up the tomatoes. You have to reduce the cut tomatoes to a red paste. You have to grow the other ingredients you want in your sauce. You have to cook the sauce. You have to cook the pasta.

A few months later, a very simple Assembler appeared. Jones acquired a copy. For his fourteenth birthday, he was given the book *Programming the Z80* and taught himself to write in Assembly by working on a game called *Bunker Maze*, which was a clone of *Scramble*, an early Konami arcade side-scroller from 1981.

Because he was dependent on the Spectrum's cassette interface, the process was unbearably slow. He'd load the Assembler. He'd load the code. He'd assemble the code. He'd save the code. He'd reset the machine. He'd load the compiled result and test his game. Repeat into infinity.

By the autumn of 1983, he'd finished *Bunker Maze* and demoed it for a local company. They showed an interest. Jones gave the company his master tapes. When he asked for them back, the company had lost the game.

•

His next program was one that would greatly impact his later titles. A graphics program called *The Palette*, Jones describes it as a "proto-Photoshop" which allowed him to construct the animations for *Go to Hell* and *Soft & Cuddly*. He describes a stunning process: "I would be able to draw each animated frame, often by literally sticking tracing paper of my sketches across the television, and following with a draw cursor."

The Palette had distinctive fill patterns, which allowed for shading, and excellent color control, letting Jones maneuver around the Spectrum's distinctive ink-and-paper bleed and create the illusion of hi-res graphics.

He sold The Palette to a company called Llainlan Software, a Welsh publisher also known as Reelax Games, in 1984.[21] [22] He received a £20 advance and used the money to buy a better Assembler, which is what allowed him to code and compile Go to Hell and Soft & Cuddly.

---

21   In late 1985 or early 1986, Reelax would release One Bite Too Deep, a sort-of kind-of horror game for the Commodore 64 that bears some resemblance to Go to Hell, if the latter title were stripped of all value, personality, and aesthetic interest.

22   The cassette inlay of Soft & Cuddly contains a "Programmer Profile" of John George Jones, which lists his previous software releases. The Palette and something called Sky Warrior are attributed to Jones and said to have been published "Llainlansoft." When asked about Sky Warrior, John George Jones replied, "Sky Warrior is a bit of a mystery to me too—perhaps it was The Power House's marketing guys getting imaginative?" Llainlan never published a title called Sky Warrior, but Reelax Games did release a title of this name in 1985. Its BASIC loader attributes the game to L.A. Wilson.

At the age of fifteen, he started work on *Go to Hell*. Jones describes the game as, "A not-too-subtle comment on my opinion of computer gaming."

Bored by the lack of horror in the computer industry, he wanted to write something that was nasty, and, as would become his trademark, actively annoying to the player. He had no intentions of selling it. It was personal entertainment.

When he finished the game, he brought it to his local W.H. Smith and showed it on a floor model Spectrum. An employee of the store suggested that Jones try a distributor, and apparently took it upon himself to send a copy (not the master tape) to one of his contacts.

Months later, what Jones describes as "a certain large unnamed software company, still very active in the industry and with whom I still have a contract an inch thick," invited him to their London headquarters. (Across several emails and a more formal interview, Jones has refused to identify Activision, or any other firm, as the company in question.)

They wanted to talk about the game.

The rest is history.

6. WE ALL WANT OUR TIME IN HELL

FIRST THINGS FIRST: The cover is a masterpiece. Atop a solid white background, the gothic typeface from *Alice Cooper Goes to Hell* has been duplicated and reduced to the words "Go to Hell."

In the Cooper original, the right horizontal bar of the *H* has a descender. On the cover of *Go to Hell*, this has been colored red. Three drops of blood fall from it. At the bottom of the cover is a pool of blood.

It's stark, it's minimalist, and it passes the only real test of design: It still looks excellent, decades later, without any reliance on nostalgia.

•

The game's manual, tucked inside the cassette case, is printed on a double-sided scrap of paper. The text describes both the gameplay and the storyline:

ABANDON HOPE
ALL YE WHO ENTER HERE…
Dante's Inferno
(Or: WELCOME TO MY NIGHTMARE)

You ought to watch your temper. You shouldn't have argued with your best friend, and told him to go to hell. Even though you didn't know that Judgment Day was nigh…

He's there now, suffering the torments of the damned. And you damned him. But life is just: You are offered the chance of redemption for your conscience, and your friend's soul. All you have to do is go and save him. You have to Go to Hell…

No mortal can prevail unaided against the wiles of Satan. Heavenly help has been provided in the form of seven sacred crosses, scattered throughout the dark realm. Dropped into the very centre of Hell's maze, you must explore the passages, find and collect the power in the six crosses, then search out the seventh cross in Beezlebub's own lair and confront him with the power of good…

Satan isn't going to give up your friend without a fight, though. His maze offers death at every turn. Demonic pitchforks writhe, eager to impale your flesh. Living walls throb in anticipation, hoping to drain your soul's energy. Molten rivers await a chance misstep. All around you, the damned are being stretched on racks, sawn apart, having their skulls crushed for eternity. Rows of bells sound the death knell, dragons' teeth seek to rend you.

But that's only the start. The Devil's minions have been turned loose to chase and kill. Spiders lay a silken trail of death. Gravestones, gallows and guillotines pursue you. Axes and pitchforks fly around. Mad monks and disembodied heads and eyes seek you out. Clouds of spirits, torn from the dead, float after you. All of them are hurling daggers at you in your travels. Only the skillful throwing of crucifixes can destroy them and their weapons. Touching them drains your energy.

Satan permits you three attempts. Fail, and you join your friend in Hell—forever...

In the early 8-bit era, games were so primitive that companies were behooved to provide exterior narratives to help make sense of the experience. Unless the titles were homebrew, these explanations were rarely written by the people who wrote the source code.

So, yes, there is a narrative of *Go to Hell* about sending your friend to Hell and staging a rescue mission. It's certainly what was reported upon in the gaming press, and continues to be recycled on the Internet.

But within the game itself, there's no evidence for any of this.

Go to Hell is something else, something stranger.

•

With every Spectrum game, there was an interminable delay between pressing PLAY on your cassette deck and the game fully loading. To pass the time, game developers often included loading screens, static images into which the user could stare as the magnetic head read data from the tape.

Go to Hell's loading screen was drawn by John George Jones using *The Palette*. The image is atop a black background. At its left is a cliffside with a gallows erected upon it. The letters "AC" are carved into the cliffside, which we assume are a reference to Alice Cooper, but could stand as easily for Adult Contemporary or Air Conditioning or Aleister Crowley. Blood pools on the precipice. Beneath the cliff, we encounter one of John George Jones's visual trademarks: a complete disinterest in perspective and scale, embodied in the form of a bloody axe about half the size of the cliff.

At the opposite side of the screen is another cliff, also bloodied, with a guillotine floating to its left. A yellow bucket is positioned beneath the guillotine. A trail of blood is leaking from its bottom. We presume the bucket has caught the head of a historical personage. Perhaps Charlotte Corday.

Hovering above the right cliff are skeletal hands holding a mutilated body by its legs. It's the source of the blood. Beneath the axe are the words: "Author / J. Jones." Beneath the right cliff are the words: "666 / Triple Six."

At the center top of the image is its title: *Go to Hell*, in the same typeface as the cover. At the center bottom is the green-faced Alice Cooper from the cover of *Alice Cooper Goes to Hell*, red flames rising off his verdant visage.

Remember what John George Jones wrote about *The Palette*. He would draw something onto paper, tape it to his television, and trace it with his software.

When we look at this loading screen, we are encountering prime evidence of capitalism's ability to eat anything. We are seeing a multinational corporation commercializing the notebook of a fifteen-year-old.

•

The game loads. The screen goes black. The Triple Six logo appears, then blanks out, then the word PRESENTS appears, then blank, then the game's title appears in the familiar typeface. Then blank again.

Now comes a much larger version of Alice Cooper's face. Above and below him are iterations of the game's title. Alice is winking and smiling in a crude two-frame animation. The effect is deeply unsettling, like being leered at by a lip-licking pervert on 14th Street.

John George Jones offered some background on this image, indicating it was the genesis of the game:

> I was messing about with the *Palette* program and did a sketch that was a fair impression of Cooper on the *Goes to Hell* album. After a bit of work making sure the colours didn't clash, I managed to get a reasonable likeness—then (I was pretty obsessive with ideas when I got them) I wanted to animate the image, so I wrote some code to flick between two versions of it on the screen.
>
> I immediately ran into problems, because the really very slow Spectrum couldn't print the image fast enough to not have it look really glitchy. (I wasn't even thinking a game at this point.)
>
> I went into the code, and stripped everything down to a minimum number of operations, (XOR A (1 instruction) instead of LD A,'0'-1

instruction plus data load for example) but this was still really inadequate.

Eventually I hit on the idea of having no loops, but simply have in memory all the instructions up to a maximum length (printing the full screen in height & width) and before calling the routine, the memory of the code itself would be poked at the right point with a jump instruction so loops and their conditional checks could be eliminated and the width & height of the character—I learnt later in University what an apparent programming faux pas this is, but it worked, and worked really well, it was just much, much faster.

When the user grows tired of Alice Cooper's winking, they can press any key and be prompted to choose their method of input. Keyboard or joystick. Once this is selected, a black screen presents a single-line message in a spindly typeface: "AUREVOIR OR IS IT GOOD-BYE?"

The screen blanks again and then the user finds his avatar in a tableau of the dankest netherworld. The avatar is a crude icon not much removed from a stick figure.

Bright red spikes emerge from brick walls. Skulls expand and contract their eye sockets. The blade of a guillotine moves up and down, up and down. Rows of tiny devils scrape and bow, gyrating their pitchforks. Miniature white men do the backstroke in a blue river situated atop the scrolling, repeating letters: H0H0H0. The rock walls of Hell pulsate, gyrate, and twist. A giant red dragon is in repose near the bottom, opening and closing its mouth, all teeth and eyes.

And that's just the first screen.

There are over 50 more.

•

The lack of perspective or scale—where a Gary Panter punk head five times the size of your avatar can exist, happily, beside a miniature man hung on a gallows and an oversized pair of eyes borrowed from T. J. Eckleburg—ends up being the game's biggest strength. Through the alchemy of contrasting size, *Go to Hell* really does convey a sense of infernal enormity. The realm of the damned loops back on itself endlessly. You can wander forever, dodging the yo-yo skulls attached to gallows until the end of everything.

As you make your way through Hell, you are subject to two types of attack: (1) Free-floating entities like spiders, ghosts, and miniature gallows, some of which throw hypodermic syringes. (2) Accidentally touching anything.

Everything is toxic. The walls, the monsters, the architecture—it all drains your life with the slightest touch. These are the situations so memorably described in the manual: "[Satan's] maze offers death at every turn."

The tight maneuvering combined with the assaults of the free agents make *Go to Hell* very difficult. Each time you die, you're returned to the first screen. All of your hard work is reduced to nothing. There are no extra lives. There are no power-ups. You have three chances before game over and you're booted out with the message, "IT'S GOODBYE."

The gaming press's many middling reviews bemoaned that beyond the unique visuals, there was nothing new on display. "In the end, no amount of grizzly graphics will convince me that this is anything other than a fairly average maze game," wrote S.D. for *Home Computing Weekly*.

•

The mistake is believing that *Go to Hell*'s pleasures derive from its gameplay, as if we're all jonesing for just one more iteration of an Italian stereotype hopped up on magic mushrooms and committing acts of cultural appropriation by dressing in ritualistic animal suits as he makes his way to Coachella.

The strength of video games has never been in their ability to convey character and plot. (And who knows, really, asks the professional writer, what either word means?)

The virtue of *Go to Hell* is its succession of disjointed images, the combined effect of a sentient axe chasing you through the pits of Hell while you touch blinking crosses and watch oversized heads being smashed.

We're in the territory of what used to be called avant-garde cinema, that beautiful moment in the 20th century when filmmakers like Buñuel and José Mojica Marins, raised in Catholicism, employed overt Judeo-Christian imagery to produce visceral thrills. The sensation of the signifier disconnected from its natural relationship to other signifiers, tempting us to reject the full range of sin's imaginary consequences.

•

The problem starts with the title. *Go to Hell* sounds very descriptive until you realize that you don't go anywhere. You start in Hell. You never leave Hell. There is no sense of why you're there or how you got there. You could be a visitor or you could be the damned.

It's not even clear that you are in Hell. Nothing in the game indicates that its gameplay takes place in the underworld. Maybe you're in the world's worst sex club, rivaling even North Hollywood's Lair de Sade.

Your only cue is that Alice Cooper—and here we assume that it's Cooper speaking but there's no actual indicator of this—has wondered whether it's aurevoir [sic] or good-bye. Why, exactly, Alice Cooper would be interested in the linguistic distinction between a farewell in French and one in English is never explained.

Maybe things in Hell are that boring.

Or maybe Cooper's that debauched.

It's important to note that the figures named in the manual make no appearances. There is no Satan or Beezlebub. Perhaps someone in the legal department decided that mentioning Cooper might invite litigation. So the shock-rocker becomes the Lord of Flies. But in the game itself, it's undeniable. There's only one major figure. The disembodied leering face of AC.

As you wander through the blasted landscape, you notice that blinking crosses are scattered across the map. Each cross is a different color. When you touch a cross, a smaller representation of that cross appears in your sidebar. In the inherited language of video gaming, we know this to mean that you've collected a cross and it now resides in your inventory.

But the in-game crosses never disappear. Have you actually collected them? What if something else has happened? What if you are undergoing an experience of transformation? What if touching a cross brands you with its mark?

When you've completed the nigh-on impossible task of collecting all six crosses, you proceed to Alice Cooper's nook. There's a seventh cross beside his head.

You can stand here for as long as you'd like, waiting for all eternity. This is the only screen where no enemies will assault you. When the moment arrives, and you decide to brand yourself with the seventh cross, the screen clears, momentarily, before flashing through all the colors of the Spectrum in a *grand mal* inducing flurry.

And then comes the message, in that same spindly font as aurevoir or good-bye: WELL DONE, YOU ARE AS SICK AS ME!

•

There are three Alice Coopers. There's the man beneath the makeup, Vincent Furnier. There's Alice Cooper, the band. And there's Alice Cooper, the persona adopted by Furnier. The one who loves the dead. The one on stage with the guillotine.

That's the real Alice Cooper. The thought of Alice Cooper. The dream of Alice Cooper.

Let's assume that *Alice Cooper Goes to Hell* is a literal title and that the real Alice Cooper did go to Hell.

If that's the case, he'd been in the infernal rankworld since 1976. Down amongst the demons for nine years. Watching the damned be tortured, his eyes exhibiting all the indifference of the rock star with a pickled liver. God of the Stage. He alone knows what human beings will do when they're confronted by the truly famous. He's seen the degradation—and darlings, he's not impressed.

Allegedly, he's a man who after his September 14, 1975, gig at the Liverpool Empire demanded that six Geordie and Scouse groupies have sex with each other in their own sick and watched as the groupies did as he commanded. Allegedly, he's a man who's watched this tableau whilst playing a Bach cantata on his Theremin and feeding his semi-rabid dog overly buttered fois gras.

•

Here's a theory: Fame comes in stages.

Let's skip over the first two and suggest that the third stage of fame is enjoying the debasement of normal people. Andy Warhol seeing just how far Ondine will go. The fourth stage is boredom. Bob Dylan ignoring Soy Bomb.

What can Hell show Alice Cooper?

Nothing. He's on stage four. He has witnessed the fall of man.

And then comes *Go to Hell*.

A mystery rite, initiation into the new Eleusinian. A descent into the underworld, the hero's journey. You transform yourself with burning 8-bit crucifixes until there's nothing left of the original self.

You visit the sinister teaser, the man with a green face and a woman's name. If you make it across the treacherous maze, you present him with a being transformed by the touch of the colored cross. You receive his final benediction. The ultimate nod.

You have roused the winking disgrace from his apathy.

You have provided a new novelty to the old Caligula. WELL DONE, YOU ARE AS SICK AS ME!

•

John George Jones. The fifteen-year-old kid obsessed with Alice Cooper. The one who drew a shock rocker on his ZX Spectrum. Jones might never meet the real thing—and by 1985, Vincent Furnier's capacities for shock and horror were greatly diminished by sobriety and an embrace of Jesus—but he could recreate the old Alice, the real Alice, the Alice that everyone remembered.

And John George Jones could put it on an audio cassette and he could send it to the biggest software company in the world.

And they could publish it.

And then it could go out across the United Kingdom and the rest of the world. There could be others like him, those who would bear the brand and benediction of the real Alice Cooper, the virtual recreation, the one who isn't a Republican obsessed with golfing.

The one who went to Hell and never came back.

WELL DONE, YOU ARE AS SICK AS ME!

7. WHATEVER HAPPENED TO THE MAN OF TOMORROW?

CLIVE SINCLAIR NEVER WANTED to run a company that made computers. His twin obsessions, from the days of Sinclair Radionics, were electric cars and miniature televisions.

The computers were something of an accident, brought on by the unexpected success of the MK14. That system was masterminded not by Sinclair himself but by Chris Curry, the person put in charge whilst the boss dealt with the early company's fallout.

By all accounts, Sinclair saw the profits from microcomputers and realized they were a way of moving ever closer to the really important projects.

Which, again, were electric cars and miniature televisions.

•

The follow-up to the ZX Spectrum, the ZX83, became the Sinclair QL. The QL stood for Quantum Leap. Designed as Sinclair's entry into the business market, it used the Motorola 68008 as its CPU, and was thus incompatible with the Z80-powered Spectrum and its library of software.

The marketing and press around the QL made it clear that it was a clean break from the Spectrum. The old system was for the kiddies. This one's for Daddy.

Announced in 1983, the QL was released in early 1984. In a depressing repeat of the Spectrum debacle, Sinclair Research was unable to fulfill orders within the promised 28-day window.

At its launch, the QL did not exist in any meaningful sense. Not one functional computer had been built by launch day. When the early machines did arrive, they came with a cartridge hanging out of the back—called a dongle—on which Sinclair Research had stuck one-third of the OS. A large percentage of the units simply did not work. At all.

The QL was being developed as it rolled off the assembly lines. Its on-board ROM changed from week to week. Later models were incompatible with earlier ones.

It was a complete disaster.

•

It'd be easy to assume that the Sinclair QL alone destroyed the company, but there were other misadventures. The TV80, a miniaturized television with a 2" screen, announced in 1980 but not launched until 1983, took five years of development and cost over £4M.

There were problems with distribution.

The television failed.

•

Another disaster was the Spectrum+, another 1984 launch. It was the ZX Spectrum's motherboard stuck into a plastic case reminiscent of the QL.

Production problems. Unfulfilled sales. Systems that didn't work.

Doom.

•

In March 1983, when Sinclair Research was at the heights of its success, its imaginary valuation on the unlisted securities market was £126M. (The equivalent of £380M/$584M in 2016.) Sinclair made a deal to sell almost £13M worth of his stake in Sinclair Research. That same month, he used the proceeds to found a new company called Sinclair Vehicles Ltd.

The new company's sole purpose was building an electric car.

Manufacturers were engaged. The chassis was designed. Money was spent.

What Sinclair ended up with was the C5. The nicest thing that you can say—which is often the nicest thing one can say about Clive Sinclair's products—is that the vehicle looked amazing. Thirty years later and it still looks like a visitation from the far off future, the absolute heights of 80s design, like Arcee and Megatron had a baby and everyone got drunk on motor-oil at its robotic christening.

Looks aren't everything. The C5 was an electrically assisted pedal bicycle with a recumbent seat. It had very limited battery life. It didn't go above 15km/h. Everyone who saw it—everyone who wasn't working for Sinclair, anyway—immediately thought that it was a death trap. It was a tiny tricycle, made of plastic, intended to share the roads with lorries.

In *The Sinclair Story*, a 1985 biography-cum-history of Sinclair and his companies, Rodney Dale describes attending the press launch for the C5. The date was January 10, 1985.

Dale, in his role as Sir Clive's hagiographer of the moment, attended as a Sinclair booster. He describes talking to a reporter after the stage presentation:

How will the press receive this? I pick someone at random. 'Have we seen history being made today?'

'Yes, but not in the way that Sinclair hopes for. It's a shame that this vehicle could destroy credibility for the future when Sinclair comes up with real vehicles... A lot of people are going to view it, I think, as a toy rather than a serious vehicle to use on the road. And I'm worried about the road safety aspect, and I think a lot of other people are... This is a gamble, you're playing with lives—young people out on the roads... I still think it's too great a risk to allow 14-year-olds on the roads in this one—I've got a 14-year-old son... Imagine trying to cross lanes on a dual carriageway to turn right.'

It couldn't have happened at a worse time. The 1983 Christmas season had been the biggest moment in British microcomputers, generating tens of millions of pounds. The 1984 Christmas season, in which Sinclair Research invested huge amounts of money, turned out to be a bust for every computer manufacturer. The audience for micros had dried up.

Sinclair Research fell into heavy debt. Summer of 1985 was marked by talk of a takeover by Robert

Maxwell, publisher of the *Daily Mirror*, who at that very moment was robbing his employees' pension funds.

The takeover was scrapped when Sinclair instead announced a deal with Dixons, a high-street consumer electronics chain. While it gained Sinclair Research £10M, the deal had the side effect of delaying the launching of the Spectrum 128K. Dixons had stockpiled the Spectrum+. The deal was closed with the contingency that Sinclair not make any moves which would affect sales of the earlier system.

Developed in tandem with Investrónica, the Spanish distributor of the Spectrum, the 128K featured better sound, a monitor port, MIDI capacity, expanded memory, a much improved keyboard. It was the first significant upgrade of the Spectrum since its original 1982 models.

But it was still a Sinclair machine. There were quirks. The expanded memory was difficult to use. There was no joystick port.

The Spectrum 128K wasn't released until February 1986, after Sinclair endured another disastrous Christmas.

•

The C5 was a total failure. By the November of 1985, Sinclair Vehicles entered into voluntary liquidation. Only 9,000 units had sold.

•

In April of 1986, it was announced that the Sinclair computer line and its brand name were being sold to Amstrad, a rival company run by Alan Sugar.

The cost?

Five million pounds sterling.

Things had gotten so bad, and Sinclair's image was so tarnished, that it isn't clear whether Amstrad spent the money because they believed the Spectrum had any inherent value in and of itself, or because five million pounds was a cut-rate price at which to buy complete control of the low-end computer market in Britain.

With the Spectrum under their thumb, Amstrad had no competition.

Clive Sinclair and Sinclair Research were out of the micro business.

8. THE FALL OF COMMUNISM AND THE ŁÓDŹ CITY CODERS

JOHN GEORGE JONES SAYS that *Go to Hell* sold well: "I'm told, in part because of a reaction to the label name, rather than the game, the parent company was reticent [to release more titles under Triple Six] even though the game itself did pretty well."

On the other hand, one of the very few things the Activision UK staff remember is the title underperforming. Rod Cousens: "I do not believe the game was a commercial success. It sold poorly…" Roger Large: "I think we set up the dummy label Triple Six to try to stir up some controversy with the media but my recollection is that the title tanked."

But the sales figures are only one metric.

•

Consider those unlicensed Spectrum clones, all of the machines sold throughout the Soviet Union and the Eastern Bloc in numbers so great that any estimate is impossible. The two best-known models are the Pentagon and the Scorpion, but there were hundreds of different clones. Some 100% compatible, others incorporating new features. Machines with names like Didaktik Gama, Leningrad 1, Hobbit, and Moskva 48.

From the perspective of the West in 2016, where electronics built with the sweat of the poor are discarded like soiled tissue, the clones experienced an incomprehensible longevity. People used the systems for decades. The Pentagon was manufactured into the 2000s.

And these systems needed software.

Unlike the professional bootleggers of Britain, where the focus appears to have been credible one-for-one copies of Spectrum titles, pirates in the Eastern Bloc distributed software in compilations.

A 90-minute cassette could hold a number of games. You copied a title, fast forwarded a little bit, and then copied another onto the same tape. When you ran out of tape, you flipped to Side B and repeated the process.

Thousands of compilations circulated throughout Eastern Europe. Again, the numbers are beyond estimation. We know that *Go to Hell* was amongst the games circulated. We know this because it appears on multiple compilation tapes.

1 Nosferatu
2 Goto Hell
3 Friday 13th
4 Pyracurse
5 Tenebrarum
6 Terrometer

1 Werewelves
2 Zombie
3 Ghost Busters 2
+Blocks

60 SPECTRUM
Road Play

БОРЬБА с ПРИВИДЕНИЯМИ

To the surprise of no one, Friday the 13th *on the ZX Spectrum manages to be worse than even the dreaded NES version.*

Broadly speaking, 1994 was a pretty good year for candles in Russia.

We're only given as much as the heart can endure.

The leering face on the third tape is John George Jones's rendering of Alice Cooper, the one that inspired *Go to Hell*. The tape in question was the 146th compilation released by a St. Petersburg piracy organization named MIM, an acronym standing for "Михаил и Михаил" or "Mikhail and Mikhail."

The first tape was most likely made somewhere around 1989. The second tape states on its cover that it's from 1994. *MIM* #146 was issued in 1996. Eleven years later, *Go to Hell* was still in circulation.[23] [24]

•

We now turn to the year 1989 and the Polish city of Łódź.[25]

---

23 A review of all available cassette inlays on the Internet shows no evidence that *Soft & Cuddly* made it to Central and Eastern Europe. But the absence of evidence blah blah blah.

24 We should mention that *Go to Hell* had a full Spanish conversion. It appeared as *Averno* in the May 1986 issue of *Spectrum Load'N'Run,* a magazine that came with cover tapes full of software.

25 The name Łódź confuses Americans as its pronunciation (something like: "Wootz") bears no apparent resemblance to its spelling, and as all rational people know, the Latin alphabet wasn't invented to suffer the abuse of Slavs. God invented the Latin Alphabet so that Americans would have a way to confuse homonyms on placards about Sharia law.

Poland in 1989 was one of those points in history when it feels as if the world is spinning off its axis. In the span of one year, the Polish People's Republic suffered a constitutional crisis, the Poles held a more-or-less democratic election, the Communists lost control, the country rejected its status as a satellite state, and the Soviet Empire fell to pieces beneath the weight of its own bad decisions. (Not the least of which was an ill-considered war in Afghanistan.)

Against this backdrop, a 25-year-old man named Jacek Michalak was programming a pair of music demos for the ZX Spectrum. We know that Michalak was from Łódź because he had a tendency to include his address in his Spectrum demos.

91-140 Łódź City ul. Grabieniec 11A/51 Blok 265.

Grabieniec Street hosts a large number of high-rises done in the architectural style favored by Communist nations and Arab dictators. Uniform buildings in the middle of nowhere, subdivisions of despair.

So there was Jacek Michalak. His country was falling apart and building itself back up. Forty-four years of Communist rule were coming to an end. And Michalak was coding his demo, which was split into parts. Part I and Part II.

The title of both?

Go to Hell.

Go to Hell, the demo, Part I, uses the loading screen from John George Jones's *Go to Hell*. It's the same visual as the game. The two cliffs, Alice Cooper's face, the title, the bloody axe. Beneath the image, Michalak has added the text: "1-CHANGE J. MICHALAK 1989 ŁÓDŹ".

The 1-CHANGE indicates the demo's purpose, which is to showcase music that Michalak has coded for the AY-3-8910 chip of the Spectrum 128K, a drastic improvement on the original beeper of the early model Spectrums. Each time that the user presses 1, a new song begins.

Michalak's only other alteration is to have animated three elements of John George Jones's original drawing. The hangman's noose twists in a repeating circle. Alice Cooper's eyes are now animated, their pupils moving left to right. And the guillotine's blade now shudders up and down.

The latter two elements contain an innovation of Michalak's: Their motion is synched with variations in the music.

•

Go to Hell, Part II, begins in the same way as John George Jones's *Go to Hell*. Blank screens and: TRIPLE SIX /

PRESENTS / *GO TO HELL*. Michalak has changed the color of all the lettering to purple. And then, as with the original, we are confronted by John George Jones's giant face of Alice Cooper. Green and leering.

Michalak has synced music to two giant guillotines, one on each side of Alice Cooper's head. As the demo plays, the blades rise and fall with changes in the sound.

The other new element which Michalak has introduced is a scrolling text marquee at the bottom of the screen. It reads:

JACEK MICHALAK PRESENTS 'GO TO HELL PART II' YOU MAY PRESS 1 TO CHANGE TUNE MUSIC COMES FROM 'WIZBALL' 'VENOM' 'BATMAN' 'DNA' HELLO HACKERS CAT-MAN, JOHN SAPER (GENS3?), KASSOFT, CHRIS (KNIGHT LORE II), SZAFRAN (AMIGA) TO MOJE DRUGIE I OSTATNIE DEMO BYE!

TO MOJE DRUGIE I OSTATNIE translates as "This is my second and last." But *Go to Hell* Part II was not Michalak's final demo. As part of the Łódź City Coders, he would contribute dozens more demos over the next few years. His last effort was released in 1994.

In an interview for this book, Michalak was asked if, while he was coding his demos, he paid any attention to the Polish political situation in 1989.

Not at all. I always stay away from politics, so after I finished my day job, I returned home and wrote demos for ZX all day long.

This is the only sane answer to any political upheaval. The ancient Greek philosopher Epicurus, the smartest man who ever lived, made it a specific point in his recipe for a happy life: "Live hidden." Pay no attention to politics or to the current trends of the day, Epicurus recommends, and avoid, at all costs, being noticed.

But from another perspective, there is revelation in Michalak's disconnection from the biggest event in post-WWII Polish history in favor of programming his ZX Spectrum. It was, after all, a computer from the West, and not just any Western country, but from England, a country run by Margaret Thatcher, one of the era's major anti-Communist crusaders.

A year before the release of the *Go to Hell* demos, Thatcher had staged a visit to the Polish city of Gdansk, where she visited with the leaders of the Polish resistance movement, Solidarność.

This visit's effects are highly debatable, but the reality is that the woman was there, lecturing the country's dissidents in arch tones about the Virtues of Freedom: "If you have a free society under rule of law, it produces both dignity of the individual and prosperity."

All of which sounds fine, until we recall that Thatcher's vision of a Free Society wasn't so much about the freedom of the individual as it was about the freedom of elites to practice and prosper from unregulated capitalism visitations upon the individual. Let's not forget that this is the Iron Lady who touted her government's role in Clive Sinclair's success by boasting about producing a general anxiety in Britain's parents.

Michalak's indifference to the Fall of Communism and to the total reordering of global politics can be read as something beyond the anonymous life of an Epicurean. It's the Spectrum working to its full effect.

Thatcher embraced the system, in part, because it functioned along the lines of imperialism. Why else would she have thrown it in the face of Japan's Prime Minister?

The computer and the console are not ideologically neutral. Like any technology, they carry the prejudices and political leanings of their creators.

Stealth imperialism comes in 8-bit color.

9. AFTER SEVEN CHAPTERS, THE RE-EMERGENCE OF *SOFT & CUDDLY*, THE APPARENT TOPIC OF THIS BOOK

THE FIRST AND ONLY FORMAL in-print interview with John George Jones appeared in issue #67 (October 1987) of *Sinclair User*. Due to demands of the newsstand, the cover date bears no real resemblance to the magazine's time of release. From the content, it seems a safe guess that it was published after the *Star* denounced *Soft & Cuddly* on August 26.

The interview was part of a feature called "C.O.D.E. T.A.L.K" in which *Sinclair User* interviewed programmers.[26]

---

26 A full examination of the *Sinclair User* run has not been made, but we may assume that all the interviewed programmers were men. The early microcomputer scene was dominated by boys. When a woman did appear, she was subject to some real bullshit. Both *Crash* and *Zzap!64* were appalling on the topic of Activision's Claire Hirsch, and let us say nothing of the Hannah Smith, *Crash*'s "Girlie Tipster," and her mud-wrestling fiasco. *C'est la guerre.*

A photo of Jones accompanies the interview. He sports a wonderful 1980s mullet, and his eyes are ringed with dark eye shadow. In the foreground are three windup toys from AmToy's *MadBalls* line.[27]

JOHN GEORGE JONES

If ever there was a controversial programmer in years gone by, you can bet that he wasn't as controversial as the author of Go to Hell **and now** Soft and Cuddly **from the Power House. Manically egotistically psychotic or a fairly nice bloke? Read on and decide for yourselves . . .**

A person can be one of two things: a manically egotistical psychotic or a fairly nice bloke. Gaming never changes.

---

27 Two Horn Heads and one Skull Face. Half a year later, the official *MadBalls* video game would be released for the ZX Spectrum and other microcomputers. It was mediocre.

Even though the Hungerford Massacre goes unmentioned, the interview highlights the media persona Jones had adopted in the tragedy's wake:

Q. It says on the cassette inlay that you're a singer/songwriter. How did you get involved with computers, then?

A: What star sign are you? What year were you born? Leo, eh? They're usually tossers, but I think you may be OK. Anyway, going a long way back, I wrote this art program and took it round to lots of people, and a few said they were interested, and then they turned around a month or so later and just said, "Who are you?" So I wrote *Go to Hell* as a kind of reply to them.

Q: Whatever possessed you to write *Soft & Cuddly*? It's pretty horrible.

A: It was much more disgusting in the original version. The babies in the game were originally being ripped apart, and the sheep bouncing up and down on a corpse. I didn't write the game because I'm a horrible person, I wrote it to amuse myself. I love the reaction people give. I can't stand 'nice' inoffensive things, like Jimmy Tarbuck and *Terry and June*. They drive me up the wall.

Q: I don't suppose there are many programmers or programs around that you like much at the moment, then?

A: No. They're all rubbish. Everything ever written has been useless. Like when *Jet Set Willy* appeared, everyone screamed 'Hallelujah!' but it was nothing. My game is the best game ever written. You should have given it ten stars.

Q: What sort of place do you live in, John?

A: Exeter. It's a horrible place. But I live with my girlfriend Wendy and she's a Pisces and she's very cuddly. I have a rabbit named Abau Chanab. My dad invented the name, because it sounded stupid…

Q: What annoys you most?

A: Games players, I think. They should be shot. I hate false modesty too…

Q: How long do you think you'll be interested in computers?

A: I've already lost interest. Most of the people who use them are boring. Hackers are just totally sad. *Soft & Cuddly* is for people who are bored with the other lousy games, and want something new…

·

Despite the insistence of desperate PhD candidates, the vast majority of games are meaningless. This is by design. You can do anything in *World of Warcraft* except express meaningful, substantial doubts about the capitalist underpinning of the experience.

But a few exceptions do slip through.

One of the unsung heroes of the Spectrum was Chris Sievey, a songwriter who later achieved modest fame as the terrifying Mancunian novelty act Frank Sidebottom. (You might have seen the 2014 film *Frank*, very loosely based on Sievey's act.)

Before he donned the papier-mâché head, Sievey released several pieces of software for Sinclair systems. The best known is *The Biz*, a music business simulator as written by an industry malcontent. Another was a music video, programmed by Sievey in BASIC, included on the B-Side of his 1983 *Camouflage* 7" single. (The first CGI music video, whatever the accolades thrown upon Dire Straight's "Money for Nothing.")

In the *SU* interview, John George Jones was asked about the music that he liked. His answer went some way towards expressing the proper feeling: "Peter Hammill is great. He was in a band called *Vandergraph* [sic] *Generator* and he invented punk, not John Lydon."

And there's the word. *Punk*. The simplest distillation of the essence. The thing missing from almost every computer game of the 1980s. The reason why Sievey put on Frank Sidebottom's head.

In the early days, owning a microcomputer was its own subcultural identity. If you had a Spectrum, you didn't need to be a punk, a goth, a Los Angeles Deathrocker, or a New Romantic. The outside world could be ignored. Shades of Jacek Michalak. The interiority of programming, the wonders of the autodidact, the QWERTY tetrapharmakos.

In its innocence, *Go to Hell* is not punk. There's just not enough attitude, not enough of a willingness to go beyond the far extremes of taste. It's still playing by the rulebook.

Something happened between *Go to Hell* and *Soft & Cuddly*.

It isn't hard to imagine what. The disappointment of the artist whose first work fails to set the world aflame.

So the biggest software company in the world has published you? What did it get you? A dummy label with a fake address? A bit of dosh and some shitty reviews written by idiots? So what's the solution, what's the answer?

Why not a game that spits in the face of the morons who wrote the rulebook? Why not a game that's genuinely, actually, punk?

10. H.E.X. MAGICK WITH THE ELEMENTAL WOMAN

THE POWER HOUSE PUBLISHED CRAP. No one imagined that its titles were helping the faded flower of England rise and bloom again.

Other than *Soft & Cuddly,* the firm's only lasting contribution was what it did with its audio cassettes, which was use the blank space after the games to include songs written and performed by an outlet called the House Electronic Xperience (H.E.X.)

The idea was Andy Wood's:

Wayne Allen and I were in a band together (a duo at the time)—Kick Partners, whilst at Nottingham Trent University. We wrote and recorded [the song included with *Soft & Cuddly*] then. I did play drums on it and co-wrote the lyrics…

I felt that the empty side of Spectrum and Commodore 64 cassette tapes were wasted. I had some of our old recordings mastered on to them for added entertainment (maybe a little pioneering spirit) and to give a little extra value to the user. Wayne Allen was helping in the warehouse at this time, so it was easy to initiate.

Wayne Allen was the central figure of H.E.X., the sole person to help write and perform all of its songs. Whilst the group shared much of its DNA with Kick Partners, which in its later incarnation was championed by John Peel and featured on his 16 March 1983 radio show, Allen is adamant that the two projects were separate:

H.E.X. wasn't Kick Partners under another name. It was a different project altogether. However the songs were recorded over a period of time and Andy and I were founder members of Kick Partners and set up H.E.X. as entirely separate project. Kick Partners was a reggae band with up to eleven members at times, but only Andy and I were involved in H.E.X. apart from a couple of songs that featured Rose Eyre, Kick Partner's female vocalist. There was a strong reggae influence to some of the H.E.X. material but it wasn't the only influence. A lot of it had nothing to do with reggae.

"To Be an Iron Maiden," the song included with *Soft & Cuddly*, sounds different than the other H.E.X. tracks, a New Wave stomper described by Robert Fearon of *Take This Machine* as, "this sort of piledriving cod-goth thing." The first verse and chorus give some sense of its thrust:

Cloning and test tube babies
Wild life preservation
No perfume no colouring
Third degree deviation
American successful woman
Waiting for the penetration
Outdoor girl wants
Different shades of emancipation

Are you reading the right books?
Know how to put on those good looks?
Have you been liberated?
Have you read that you're fated?
To be an Iron Maiden
Well, maybe you're not

•

When asked if Mrs. Thatcher had any influence over the song, Wayne Allen replied in some detail:

"To Be a Modern Woman" was changed to "To Be an Iron Maiden" because of Thatcher and her ideology. The idea of the song came from all these headings and subheadings from women's magazines—all encouraging women to be "modern women" and powerful and independent. I wasn't saying that was wrong but I was questioning if it was right. In my youthful innocence back in the 80s I thought it was a shame that women were being encouraged to feel they didn't need men (and vice versa). It seemed that we were all being encouraged to be tough, hard individuals, looking after number one and not to care for others. I felt that women were being encouraged to be ruthless uncaring individuals who got what they wanted by whatever means necessary, and to be like Thatcher... (A bit naive maybe—but I was young when I wrote it.) [28]

---

28 Be kind. Everyone's sexual politics always look bad, and everyone's sexual politics always look bad 30 years later. The Future People are judging you, reader, for your own terrible thoughts and deeds.

As with everything, *Soft & Cuddly* was the outlier.

"To Be an Iron Maiden" is not only the best of the H.E.X tracks, but also the sole instance where the musical inclusion makes thematic sense.[29] With the song's focus on a landscape of nightmare plastic and test-tube babies, it could easily be a commissioned soundtrack matching John George Jones's visuals.

For a contrast, we might look at 1986's *Hercules*, a game in which a stick figure representation of, we assume, Herakles as he traverses one of the Spectrum's barest-bone—and neon-ugliest—*Manic Miner* clones. The game is so simple and nasty. Beyond its title and a few crude icons, there's literally no connection to its title. It's an empty void. Some old shit that someone tried shining with a mythology theme.

What's the H.E.X. track on its B-side? A soothing synth-reggae song with Rose Eyre singing about modern life and how the attentions of a lover can be used as sweet therapy to address the ennui of existence in 1980s.

---

29 For both accuracy and the utter subversion of this chapter: The Power House also released budget titles for the Commodore 64, including *Gun Runner*, which included "To Be an Iron Maiden" on its tape. The pairing is not fitting.

An individual who we will encounter in our epilogue and who has asked to be identified as Earl C. describes the effect of the pairing of "To Be an Iron Maiden" and *Soft & Cuddly:*

Soft & Cuddly the game […] is the best possible use of the ZX Spectrum's capabilities by itself; but it's when paired with his companion piece […] they are both transformed into something else. They really are two entirely separate creations I'm sure, but because they were released together they are inseparable in my mind. The game has a sort of demonic, distinctly British occult horror feel, while the track inexplicably has a ghostly, slightly gritty post-punk vibe. Mashed together, it's a sumptuous mega-British punk maniac horror pentagram hell like nothing else in the universe. They go together so powerfully that I wish it was intentional, I wish the B-side was actually somehow the backing track of the game. I hope some contemporary gamer, on some lonely and forgotten precipice in Shrewsbury, or whatever a name of some backcountry English city is, bought two tapes of *Soft & Cuddly* and played them concurrently.

11. I LOOKED INTO THE ABYSS THINKING THE ABYSS WOULD LOOK BACK INTO ME BUT I DISCOVERED THAT THE ABYSS IS AN ASSHOLE WHO WON'T MAKE EYE CONTACT

If you're coming to *Soft & Cuddly* after playing *Go to Hell*, the first thing you notice is that you are once again confronted by John George Jones's drawing of Alice Cooper.

But the image has changed. It's no longer recognizable as Alice. The face still winks, but it's been re-colored in two shades of blue: light for skin, dark for the hair. There's a green open sore on Non-Alice's forehead that leaks blood. His right eye also leaks blood. His left eye bulges out, a fully distended circle, and leaks blood.

His mouth is a red smear, the smile of The Man Who Laughs. It leaks blood. Atop his head grows a crown of spikes.

Jones has placed two monsters on either side of Non-Alice.[30] These blue creatures open and close their jaws while crunching a face between their teeth. When the faces are crunched, the monsters' jaws leak blood.

A hand-drawn logo that reads *SOFT & CUDDLY* rests beneath the three figures, surrounded on both sides by red snakes.

•

When the player tires of the leering Non-Alice, any press of a button brings up an input select screen, giving the standard choices between keyboard and joystick control.

This screen also lists the keyboard input controls, but neglects to mention that hitting "I" will turn the player invisible and invincible for a small duration of time, and instead displays the option of "(/ Lie)" followed by the letters "Lg."

---

30 In a curious synchronicity, these are located in the same spots that Jacek Michalak placed guillotines in *Go to Hell* Part II.

In the game, the (/Lie) command does nothing. As we'll see, Lg are initials of some meaning.

A scrolling marquee runs along the screen's bottom. As long as the player doesn't select a method of input, they can wait and read the full text:

©L.Green&J.Jones(ex666).You are Dren the last of the kingdom of Starp, the last of the race of Snigriv, & the highest of Lauxes-serulaif of the universe, The Queen is dieing & only you, a real Dren-Ecaf can save her. Do you believe this tripe? Are you mad?? /Its time someone shot Zarf of Fex, Cronos the mole, kill em all!,/Go & Have fun Dren. Hi Alice!/[31]

This seems as good a place as any to discuss the narrative of *Soft & Cuddly*.

The cassette inlay which accompanied the game contained two narratives which have nothing to do with the one that appears in the marquee. The first narrative, on the exterior, reads:

All dead, all dead, all dead and gone.

---

31 Can you crack the crytopgraphic code of a teenager from England in the 1980s?

But this is the Cyborg Age. Kids laugh and joke on the streets and say, "we can re-build him!" Well you can, but it has to be the right mix of sinew and metal and first you have to enter the nightmare to retrieve the pieces of what spawned you.

. . . Eurgh! . . .

Horror show, horror show.

The second narrative, on the inlay interior, reads:

Your mother, The Android Queen, has been badly damaged in an accident. Your father has been locked in a fridge with evil spirits by your mother. (Nice family eh!).

You must find the eight spirit keys and exchange them for information about where the various parts of your mother are hidden. To do this, take the keys to your father in the fridge.

When all the parts of her body have been taken to the fridge, find the needle and thread so she can be sewn back together.

Whatever else happens in *Soft & Cuddly*, there are no spirit keys. There is no needle and thread. In issue #26 (February 1988) of *Your Sinclair*, the columnist Philip Snout addressed this confusion:

Oo-er! I must say, I just got a completely hat-stand (and it must be said utterly unprintable letter) from the author of The Power House's *Soft And Cuddly*, **John 'Wacko' Jones**[.] Oo-er again. It shocks even me, and I don't shock easy, matey. The bit I *can* print tells of an update to the slightly vague instructions you get with the game: "**…now this is important. (slaver, bark) The instructions are a touch misleading. (heh heh) There are no keys, but before you can get any bit of your mother you must visit the fridge first. (dribble) The fridge moves position every game. Then your decapitated dad will reveal a piece of your mother's body, (yibble yibble) it normally starts with her botty, take it back to the fridge and so on. (heavy breathing) If anyone wants to write me, feel free, I am interested in other people's opinions, even if it's just to remind me that mine are best…**" and so on for another couple of slimy pages. Worra fruitloop! Still, thanks for the tips… I think.

John George Jones's original design for a Soft & Cuddly cassette inlay under its first title Love it to Death.

If you re-read the marquee text, you'll note a copyright notice attributing the game to John George Jones and someone called "L.Green." Throughout the game, the player encounters a graphic of two conjoined twin babies. On their chest appears the word LUCY. The initials "Lg."

In an interview for this book, John George Jones talked about the original story behind *Soft & Cuddly*:

> Lucy Green is the character whose parents you are trying to reunite, after all the bits have been found and sewn back together so they can be brought back to life—The Power House toned this down to some 'Robot Queen's' dismembered body type chat—Though the underlying original story was very positive about bringing people back together and righting some injustice—but apparently the details were a bit too much for their marketing department...

Before the game even starts, four narratives have befallen the player. An argument can be made that we've entered the realm of the ontological.

If a narrative can exist, then how do we determine which of *Soft & Cuddly*'s four stories is the "real" one? Is the game about the Cyborg Age? Is it about the Android Queen? Are we playing as Dren, last of the Snigriv? Or is this the tale of

Lucy Green and her parents, characters effaced by rounds of revision and commercial considerations?

John George Jones's games exert a power 30 years after everyone has forgotten the hundred other titles released by The Power House or its parent company CRL. There is something unique and strange about a person whose two major works were designed in such a way that it is impossible to say what, exactly, is happening.

Consider, by contrast, the gold standards, Matt Smith's *Manic Miner* and *Jet Set Willy*. Even loading the games blind, we understand the action.

Let's move even closer to the source. Back to the early days. Think about *Pac-Man*, as primitive of a game as one can imagine. The narrative is still clear. Your goal is to acquire round glowing Communion wafers while not having your Christian faith shaken by the presence of disembodied spirits, a process that occasionally requires you to don the armor of a holy warrior and defeat the evil of doubt by consuming ethereal spectres.

Okay. Maybe not.

We know that *Pac-Man* isn't about the sadomasochistic spiritual practices of Opus Dei because we can see the contrary evidence with our eyes, a luxury not present in *Go to Hell* and especially not in *Soft & Cuddly*.

If either of Jones's games were one-offs, if we were talking about one game that was resistant to the imposition of narrative, then it would be an easy discussion. *It's an accident. It's a mistake. Someone fucked up. Something got lost in translation. Something went wrong in marketing.*

When the process is repeated, then the situation is different. Do something once and you're an asshole. Do it twice and you're a genius. Beneath the gory graphics, beneath the teenaged madness, beneath the punk *fuck you* and the obsession with Alice Cooper, there is an unknowable thing.

In an email exchange, Clem Chambers, the founder and owner of CRL, the parent company of The Power House, described *Soft & Cuddly* as, "…a pretty sketchy game and if the graphics were non-shlocky it would have had no selling potential. It was definitely a piece of exploitation-ware. It's utterly naive in comparison with games that came later. […] The game wasn't up to much. To make shlock work you have to back it up with quality craft."

But this is entirely wrong.

Schlock is schlock because there is no mystery to the thing.

The heart of *Soft & Cuddly* is mystery.

What is this? Who did this? What is happening? What the fuck is going on?

12. EVERYTHING YOU EVER WANTED IS KEPT IN THE REFRIGERATOR

BUT STILL, IT'S ALSO A GAME about big dumb monsters.

•

When you tire of Non-Alice or reading the marquee text, you choose your method of input. Then the game presents you with a prompt that reads like a 5th grade love note: "SILLY WALK(Y/N)"

The silly walk is *Soft & Cuddly* at its goofiest. It makes no difference which option you choose. Your character walks the same. There is no silly walk, only a silly question about a silly walk.

Once you've made your useless choice, you start the game with your avatar standing on a grass plain. Is this the kingdom of Starp? Your avatar, much better defined than the stick figure avatar in Go to Hell, is a blue man carrying a gun and wearing something like a top hat.

The game takes place across a series of non-scrolling screens. It resembles a platformer, but your avatar's primary method of movement is flight. Each screen is static and leads through its exits to other screens.

From the first screen, you can travel in three directions: left, right or down. Left or right take you to other grassy plains. Other than the first, all of these grassy screens are identical to each other: an old tree from which hangs a dismembered corpse.

On the first screen, there is no tree or dismembered corpse. Each surface screen has an opening to the world below, but until you visit the refrigerator, your avatar can't fly over the trees. Your only option is down.

Below the surface, the unique map is nine screens high and thirteen screens wide, making a total of 117 screens. Two screens to the left of your entrance, there begins a liminal space which links what we can think of as the left side of the map to the right, an empty nothingness three screens wide. At the map's bottom, if you fall through any hole, there is a descent of three blank screens until your avatar lands on liquid red waves. The player loses control over the character and dies on the bloody sea.

The basic mechanics of the game are as John George Jones described in his letter to *Your Sinclair*. Your first goal is find the refrigerator. It doesn't actually appear at random. The refrigerator is always located at one of two predetermined places.

Once you discover the refrigerator and walk in front of it, your character's avatar turns from blue to yellow. The only practical effect of this transformation is that you can now fly above the trees on the surface. The other effect of reaching the refrigerator is that a part of your Android Mother appears somewhere in the map. These parts are found in the same place in each new game, but their order of appearance is random.

As with both your first love affair and *Go to Hell*, everything that you touch will hurt you. Enemies float around whilst firing balls of energy. Each enemy that you kill replenishes your life meter by a very tiny amount.

Every time that you find a body part, your avatar turns blue. You then return to the refrigerator and repeat the process until you collect the final part, which is always the same object in the same place. This is described in The Power House's copy as a "thread and needle" but looks more like a metallic coil.

When you find this possible thread and needle, located above one of the several Non-Alice heads that appear throughout the map, the game ends.

•

Soft & Cuddly is a refinement of *Go to Hell*. You're still traversing a subterranean environment, but now it's done in profile, and the graphics have leapt forward. The big dumb monsters can move and are much slicker. The teenaged notebook scrawlings have given way to something approaching professionalism. Everything's polished.

Sheep stomp gravestones. Big Lovecraftian vampire squids won't stop blinking. Heads are crushed by spikes while an animated tile alternates between the words YOU and DIE. Skulls wear berets. Random signs read QUO VAGON.[32] Oversized bodies are tortured in ways that are literally indescribable. The brows of skulls crack open and close again. Wagons drive around with cargo-loads of body parts that flop about like fish. Audio cassettes dance. Televisions flicker. Corpses are transformed into mush. Feet hang from the ceiling.

And as with *Go to Hell*, there is no sense of perspective. And as with *Go to Hell*, each screen is packed with movement.

Visually, it doesn't look like a Spectrum game. It appears to be from a much more powerful system. By using *The Palette* and strategic placement, Jones managed to almost completely avoid the famous color bleed.

---

32 *Quo Vagon* has no meaning in any known language. It's closest, probably, to *Quo vadis?* which is Latin for *Where are you going?*

It's hard to imagine that there's a single person who completed *Soft & Cuddly* without cheating through direct manipulation of values in the Spectrum's memory. [33]

How difficult is the game?

First off, the laser. It slowly overheats, with an onscreen meter that ranges between 0 and 50. You can fire your laser quite a bit in the zero state, but with each firing the intervals between blasts grows longer until you can no longer fire at all. And then you're just there, weaponless, waiting for the meter to tick back down from 50 to 0, which takes much longer than getting from 0 to 50.

Second, several screens are traps. You can't win *Soft & Cuddly* without first memorizing the map and remembering which screens will kill you.

Third, when you try to pick up the different parts of the Android Queen's body, they're toxic to your avatar and resist collection. You can lose all three lives standing on your mom's tits, simply trying to complete the basic purpose of the game. It's unclear if there is a way to collect the pieces without cheating. And even then it's a matter of burning through your infinite lives as you

---

33 The two known cheats for *Soft & Cuddly* allow the player to have infinite lives and a laser that doesn't overheat.

stand on an item until it disappears into your inventory, which happens at random.

Fourth, to acquire the Android Queen's skull, you have to return to the surface in a post-refrigerator yellow state, fly over several trees and drop down a hole. After entering the underworld and navigating several screens, you get on top of the skull and finally acquire it. But each time that you pick up a new body part, your avatar turns blue. And being blue means you can't fly over trees. Like existential despair, there is no apparent exit.

One of the game's innovations, which may be a first, is that its environment is destructible. Of the avatar's laser, John George Jones writes:

> I was around 16 when I started writing stuff for *S&C*—I remember having ideas for it as I was finishing off *Go to Hell*. I was particularly excited to get the laser working, though like most things, I had no idea how to make one until I tried—It ended up with the quite nice touch that the laser could do damage to walls—always bugged me that weapons never left a mark on surroundings in most games at the time.

A great deal of the environment in *Soft & Cuddly*—not just the walls—can be obliterated, opening up a different style of play than the surface strategy. No documentation mentions this.

After grabbing the Android Queen's skull, the only solution for a player who isn't cheating is to blast your way through one of the walls, obliterating it until there's a space for your character to pass through without taking any damage.

But remember, your laser is prone to overheating. Going through the wall will require at least 300 shots. So you have to stagger your blasts. While avoiding the floating adversaries. While making sure not to touch anything.

And when you do finish the game, when you make it to the end of a process that is grueling even when cheating, after you've spent untold hours mapping and hunting body parts, what is your reward?

A bleeping noise and a screen that color cycles a line of text:

Good, whip me with a banana. Lg

13. TIME ENOUGH TO SLEEP, DARLINGS

AFTER ITS BRIEF APPEARANCE in the *Star*, the mainstream press quickly forgot *Soft & Cuddly*. The scandal lingered in the gaming scene. Reviews were stupid.

"It's a pity that such a technically sound and innovative game should be dragged down by distasteful graphics and a horribly grim inlay. [...] The gameplay is repetitive," clucked *Crash*.

"It's a bit like a cross between a splatter movie and one of those strange Belgian art movies done with stop-frame photography with people in stupid poses gliding around the room, pushing chairs, etc..." sneered *Sinclair User*.

A letter from a subscriber in issue #46 (November 1987) of *Crash* expressed discomfort with *Soft & Cuddly*'s FIRST COMPUTER NASTY promotional poster, which had been distributed in the previous issue:

…On a different tack, I would like to express my views upon the poster I received in my copy of CRASH, that is the one from the Power House. I could stand the other drawings in CRASH, even *Barbarian* etc., but this poster is truly over the top. It is truly disgusting. As soon as my mother saw it, she tore it up, such was her disgust. Please no more posters (or drawings) like that, thank you!

Michael J. Brown, Ossett, W Yorks

The poor mothers of West Yorkshire!

Brown's letter drew an editorial response that heralded a forthcoming response to *Soft & Cuddly*:

The poster: I agree with you as well! The poster (for those who are not subscribers—we sometimes let software houses include posters with subscribers' copies) was for the game *Soft and Cuddly* from the Power House. I suggest you read Mel Croucher's piece on violence in computer games in the next issue of THE GAMES MACHINE, on sale from November 19, which has quite a bit to say about both the game and the poster.

Mel Croucher is the father of British computer gaming. He founded Automata, the first English company dedicated to entertainment software. Automata released two classics for the ZX Spectrum—the games *Pimania*, an exercise in marketing that involved a real world treasure hunt and a golden sundial, and *Deus Ex Machina*, the first game to feature a synchronized soundtrack and narration.

Can of Worms, one of Automata's earliest products, was a compilation of eight games released for the ZX81. It was a ripsnorting shit-kicker, as illuminated by descriptions included with the cassette:

Program 2 VASECTOMY: "V"
A useful operation. Unfortunately you, the surgeon, have got myopic vision and are blind drunk anyway. You are finding great difficulty in getting the target of your operation into focus…

Program 4 HITLER: "H"
Infuriate Der Fuhrer. Contrary to rumor, Adolf is alive and living in an old-people's-home in Cambridge. As he propels his wheelchair & meanders around the ward, he stops at random. You are going to try & give him a heart attack, by placing a whoopee-cushion under his chair by entering "1" to "9"…

Program 8 P'S & Q'S: "P"
A pathetically scatological game, involving making water into a porcelain receptacle…

The Games Machine was a sister publication of *Crash* dedicated to multisystem coverage. The periodical was not well-loved and disappeared from newsstands in 1990.[34]

Starting with its inaugural issue (October/November 1987), Mel Croucher functioned as the magazine's moral scold, writing lengthy articles that explored thorny issues in gaming through a combination of editorial writing and interviews with luminaries.

Issue #1's topic was sex and sexism in the software industry. Issue #2 (Dec/Jan 1987/1988) describes Croucher's column as "[leaving] the seamy side of software sex and [getting] to grip with computerized violence."

The article was a response to the marketing of *Soft & Cuddly*, its attendant media furore, and the scandal provoked by *Jack the Ripper*, another CRL title. The latter was a text adventure illustrated with images of attractive women smeared with blood. (They bore no resemblance to East End prostitutes of the Victorian Era.)

Jack the Ripper had been in the news because of a novel promotional strategy devised by CRL's founder, Clem Chambers. The Video Recordings Act of 1984, a piece of legislation heavily supported by Mrs. Thatcher and passed in the wake of the Video Nasties scare, required that all games with mature content receive certification from the British Board of Film Classification.

---

34 The Italian version of *The Games Machine,* which started as translations of the British version, remains in print. *Ciao, bella.*

Chambers was the first person to seek classification, realizing that the bureaucracy could generate free publicity. In November of 1987, *Jack the Ripper* earned the very first 18 Certificate issued for a video game.[35] Cue articles in the tabloids.

Considering the nature of *Can of Worms*, one might imagine Croucher would have no concerns over violence in gaming. In fact, he was known for his extreme opposition. An interview in issue #27 (April 1986) of *Crash* provides an example:

> Mel Croucher has always held strong views about shoot 'em ups: "I find violent games very unpleasant for a number of reasons. Firstly they are pathetically inadequate, because the characters depicted are still awfully basic—just pixels—and the sounds generated are squeaks and beeps and the end product has nothing to do with *Friday [the] 13th* or *Rambo*, absolutely nothing. They are dressing up hackneyed ideas. That's my first objection. Secondly, they are totally derivative. I

---

35 The website of the BBFC explains the 18 Certificate thusly: "What does the 18 symbol mean? Films rated 18 are for adults. No-one under 18 is allowed to see an 18 film at the cinema or buy / rent an 18 rated video. No 18-rated works are suitable for children."

think the computers that we have now offer tremendous freedom of expression for any concept. Thirdly I think they are socially destructive. I've been saying it for years and people are very bored with me saying it like that but I think it is very dangerous to encourage young people to believe that winning is to do with killing. I think that's extremely dangerous. We have a new generation coming who will have no qualms whatsoever about pulling the trigger in any circumstance."

It's a bit harsh to judge someone thirty years later on something that might have been said in haste, but we should recognize that Croucher's reasoning is bizarre. Is the nature of the objection that games are socially corrupting, or is it that the 8-bit graphics prevent the user from seeing the gore?

•

Reading Croucher's column in issue #2 of *The Games Machine*, one can't help be amazed by the collective star power of the people interviewed. Croucher presents a cavalcade of storied personages from both the British establishment and the gaming industry.

In order of appearance: (1) Susan Vas Dias, Principal Child and Adolescent Psychotherapist at St. Barts

Hospital, London.[36] (2) Sir Clive Sinclair. (3) Ian Stewart of Gremlin Graphics. (4) Monsignor Bruce Kent, a soon-to-resign Catholic Priest and a high-ranking member of the Campaign for Nuclear Disarmament. (5) Jeff Minter, founder of Llamasoft; (6) Jeffrey fucking Archer. (7) Priscilla Langbridge and Marianne Scarlet of St. Bride's School, a holiday resort in Burtonport, Ireland, where grown women paid money to pretend that they were schoolgirls receiving an Edwardian education. The school's software development wing had developed the text and gameplay of *Jack the Ripper*, but had nothing to do with the imagery, which was added after they turned the game over to CRL. (8) Clem Chambers of CRL. (9) Kevin Toms of Addictive Games. (10) David & Richard Darling, brothers and co-founders of Codemasters. (11) Last, Ashley Hildebrandt, managing director of The Power House, left to pick up the pieces and explain *Soft & Cuddly*.

Following the interviews, Croucher ends his piece with a bevy of platitudes, criticizing programmers (*Why not be constructive?*), magazines (*Why take money for repulsive adverts?*), and "The Trade," by which he meant the people who made and published violent video games. (*When the kids who buy your games rape you, don't complain because your product made them rapists.*)

---

36 One of the few British medical establishments, apparently, not to be used as hunting grounds by Sir Jimmy Savile.

Jeffrey fucking Archer.

If anyone best encapsulates the postmodern shift of Thatcher's reign better than the Prime Minister herself, it's Jeffrey fucking Archer.

He was the son of a con man and a newspaper columnist. He worked for five months as a beat cop. He talked his way into Oxford as a mature student, somehow extending a one-year degree into three, leaving with to-die-for political connections. He became the fourth youngest Member of Parliament, ever, and had to resign after sinking his own small fortune into a fraudulent Canadian company called Aquablast. He left politics, bankrupt, in 1974. When he was in Canada to give evidence against Aquablast, he was held for shoplifting three suits from a store, but somehow explained the problem away. Now broke, he began writing very shitty yet extraordinarily popular novels, transforming himself into a wealthy man. Current estimates are between 250M and 400M books sold. In 1985, Thatcher appointed him Deputy Party Chairman of the Conservatives. In 1986, the *Daily Star* published evidence of his relationship with a teenaged sex worker. The *Star* said he'd had sexual relations with the person in question, so Archer sued the paper, winning £500,000 in 1987, more or less at the exact moment that he would have been speaking with Croucher. In 1992, he was made Baron Archer of Weston-super-Mare. For his last political hurrah, he ran in 1999 as the Conservative candidate for Mayor of London. During the campaign, it came out that he had lied at the *Star* libel trial. In 2001, he was put on trial for perjury and perverting justice. By the end of the year, he was in prison.

From Croucher's article:

MEL – Yes, let's talk about William, your son. Do you allow your Willie to play violent video games?

JEFFREY – I'm not conscious of any violent games William has. If he had any I would not allow him to play them. Under no circumstances.

MEL – You are talking censorship, aren't you?

JEFFREY – In a democracy, you can't go too far, you have to be very careful… I know the Prime Minister is worried, and rightly so. Even if it adds one percent to anyone's life being in danger, then it should be stopped.

MEL – So you do advocate censorship. Do you think that active participation in a violent computer game is more dangerous than passively watching a video?

JEFFREY – I've never thought about it before you said it, but yes, yes it would make one powerful, which can't be a good thing.

MEL – Power isn't a good thing?

JEFFREY – Not that sort of power.

Speaking of power: Prior to founding the British video game industry, Croucher worked as an architect for Rashid bin Saeed Al Maktoum, the Emir of Dubai. The details of what Croucher did in Dubai are a bit sketchy, but if we are to believe his quasi-autobiographical book *Deus Ex Machina: The Best Game You Never Played in Your Life*, he was instrumental in the city's early development into a center of global iniquity, a place where the rich blow enormous amounts of money in a neo-colonial sub-Vegas propped up by Oil Feudalism and actual human slavery.

Unlike the violence in a video game, there is a direct link between actual, real violence and the construction and building of Dubai. We're talking about thousands of enslaved South Asians. But who cares? It looked great in *Mission Impossible: Ghost Protocol*.

That's the way it is with genuine violence. No one really gives a shit, especially when the bloodshed is state-sanctioned and beneficial to international trade. The only dissidents are the Loony Left. Everything goes on.

•

There was something about gaming. It's receded now, in an era when *Grand Theft Auto V* can make over $2,000,000,000 in sales, in a time when the average age of gamers slowly crawls into the 40s. But there was something in those early days, when production was one person in front of one computer, chugging out code. A certain worry that the world's children could be on the receiving end of a direct address from people who hadn't, in any meaningful sense, been vetted.

But who were the vetted? Think about Jeffrey fucking Archer. At the very moment he was denouncing violent games, interviewed by a man who had provided services to a feudal state, Archer was triumphing in a libel trial where his victory was predicated on the direct manipulation of fact. But why wouldn't he lie? He was the Prime Minister's communication guru, a man she believed could deliver the Conservative message to the masses through the world's media.

If Thatcher's rise was based on the Left having been very wrong about the ability of the Powers That

Be to adapt to postmodernism, then what did the microcomputer represent?

A whole new medium that no one understood, a medium requiring enormous amounts of tedious labor to master, a medium in which the rules had yet to be written.

The Video Nasties scare was the precursor. The dawning realization that the VCR was something new. Yes, it was a machine, and yes the society understood how to adapt to new machines. It had happened before, it would happen again. There's always a place for new products.

•

But the VCR presented an unexpected problem. If television and radio were useful tools, then their utility derived from controllable content. No matter how many television channels would proliferate, there'd always be someone at the stations determining what went on the air. The VCR was controlled by its home user, granting people the ability to filter out the preapproved message.

The machines of Clive Sinclair were understood—exactly, implicitly. They were just more stereos, more televisions, more British industry that could be used as propaganda. Let's get one in every school! Let's show up the Japanese with our ingenuity!

Well and good as long as no one came along and did anything gross or offensive or beyond the pale. But offensiveness was a near certainty given the kinds of people who worked in the gaming industry. Kids with no hope of Oxford or Cambridge, kids who weren't even receiving private educations.

The real offense isn't the violence of the Falklands, or the violence of Abu Dhabi. That won't drag Jeffrey fucking Archer away from his whoremongering. That won't make Sir Clive Sinclair spill his tea whilst shuddering at the bad taste of it all.

The only real horror is not violence but its depiction, and John George Jones had the bad taste to present violence not as something disturbing but as something that might be funny.

•

The moment would pass.

For a long while, technological advancement would make it impossible for a single person to build a game with any hope of penetrating into mass consciousness. There'd still be conversations about violence and sex and death and drugs in games, but the decisions that brought these games to the market would be very different. There wouldn't be one kid saying *fuck you* to everyone around him.

After *Soft & Cuddly*, John George Jones would not produce another video game. The Spectrum was a dying system and his reception had not been particularly warm. Why keep going?

For a while, Jones took some pleasure in sending missives to gaming magazines. A few were printed.

Issue #70 (January 1988) of *Sinclair User* included one of his letters. In a bit of snide editorial layout, the text appears beneath a tightly cropped picture of Non-Alice's bleeding face.

In full:

> Concerning what is probably the best game ever written—my game *Soft and Cuddly*—I have so far received a few letters of complaint from misguided people concerned about the morality of the game.
>
> I'm sick and tired of being called immoral, when I know true morality, a new sort of real love.
>
> **John George Jones**
> **Programmer**
> **Power House**

Such a letter could not go without editorial rejoinder:

> *This guy should show more humility. Yours truly will decide if a game is good or bad.*

EPILOGUE:
FUCKER GAMER SCUM GET STABBED

WHEN OLDER GAMES ARE REMEMBERED, they tend to be discussed for reasons of historical importance—a technological, sales, or cultural milestone—or feelings of nostalgia. (Remember when you were in high school and you and that one guy used to see who was best at *Super Mario Kart* and then you didn't talk to him for five years and then he died when he was 28 and the only thing you could remember about him was his performance on the Rainbow Road?)

Most games are forgotten. There's always some discussion of *Leisure Suit Larry in the Land of the Lounge Lizards*, but decades pass without word one on *Harley Davidson: The Road to Sturgis* or *Quadralien* or *Joan of Arc: Siege and the Sword*.

That's the nature of the beast, the creeping shuffle of an industry dedicated to the thrill of the new. There's always another console and one more installment of *Assassin's Creed*.

The world spins on and everyone forgets everything unless some nagging memory pulls them back.

•

And then there's John George Jones.

A creator whose games, having had no impact when they were released, now inspire no thoughts of historical importance or nostalgia. A creator whose titles were doomed to be forgotten. Flotsam destined to never become jetsam.

And yet here you are.

Reading this book.

•

Soft & Cuddly and *Go to Hell* have gone forward from their initial moment, finding the right people at the right time.

And often the found ones have been anointed with an unholy desire to create their own works. It goes beyond Jacek Michalak and Russian bootleg tapes in the 1990s. There's always more, if you know where to look.

In February of 2001, an Estonian coder calling himself moroz1999—real name Dmitri Ponomarjov—released an enhanced version of *Soft & Cuddly*. This latter-day iteration was identical to the original, but for the fact that it contained support for the General Sound card.

The General Sound card is a plug-in peripheral manufactured throughout the former Soviet Union. The device gives the Spectrum and its clones something like parity with PC sound developments circa 1992.

John George Jones's version of *Soft & Cuddly* has no in-game music. Its sound is 1-bit effects played through the Spectrum's beeper. Fire a laser, hear a little beep.

Taking advantage of the expanded hardware, moroz1999 has scored *Soft & Cuddly* with a soundtrack of what can be described, charitably, as the world's absolute-fucking-worst heavy metal. It's beyond dreadful.

That someone cared enough to do this, thirteen years after the game's release, is beautiful.

●

November 2014 saw the release of *Fucker Gamer Scum Get Stabbed*. It was authored by Earl C., the individual we encountered in the discussion of Wayne Allen's "To Be an Iron Maiden."

Fucker Gamer Scum Get Stabbed is a Microsoft Windows homebrew game programmed and designed in a week. It was created as a part of a half-hearted game jam. It ended up being the only entry, which presumably means that Earl C. won.

From the beginning, Earl C. identified *Fucker Gamer Scum Get Stabbed* as an unofficial sequel to both *Go to Hell* and *Soft & Cuddly*. When the game starts, blasting away with the unauthorized music of Smersh—a New Jersey duo who were themselves heroes of the audio cassette revolution—it's clear that we're in the hands of someone who's imbibed the aesthetics of John George Jones.

The player's avatar looks a bit like an astronaut from the 1960s, all helmet and sleek Bowie suit. The game takes place—at least part of it—in a hospital. We know this because in addition to the IV stands and plethora of toilets, several crude blinking labels that read HOSPITAL are strewn about the screens. The screaming suicidal lunatics who rush at the player, fingers crammed in their ears, also bespeak a sanitarium.

All the John George Jones imagery appears: giant heads being crushed above signs that read PUNKS DIE, weird giant monsters, floating laughing babies, skulls wearing army caps, and screens that writhe with movement.

No one's here for the gaming experience. We've come for the imagery, for the visitation into someone else's mind.

In an interview, Earl C. explained why, exactly, this particular mind was so attracted to Jones:

…As a teenager I suffered brain damage from an infectious bacteria. The most observable effect of this affliction was a sort of blurring of the senses or stimuli: At its worst point I couldn't tell the difference between feelings like being tired or thirsty. It's not that bad anymore, but there are definite lingering effects.

The main remnants of these symptoms are most pronounced in color associations, which is what initially drew me to the ZX spectrum. […] The rich, slightly off-hue colors on a stark black background really leaped out at my fucking skull. The way they're sort of gaudily mashed together with no boundaries, leaking and seeping into each other like mayo and mustard and ketchup in a disgusting dumpster, is so grotesquely, queasily, sumptuously sensual… It may seem only natural that I'd eventually discover *Soft & Cuddly* and find it as the greatest convulsion of the ravaging spectriod phantasmagoria …

The strangest thing about *Fucker Gamer Scum Get Stabbed* isn't the imagery. It's the simple fact that the game is kind of great.

Once you figure out the controls, there's really something genuine and delightful in its adaptation of *Soft & Cuddly*'s mad worldview, moving your avatar through a neon landscape while under a constant audio-visual assault. It's a pleasure that seems inimical to John George Jones's games, which were above all else exercises in torturing the player.[37]

It's the iteration, the echo which gives us a real hint about the nature of *Go to Hell* and *Soft & Cuddly*. How many other barely-known games have inspired derivative works based not on their gameplay or an identification with characters, but rather from an interest in the underlying aesthetics?

That's the way it works, supposedly, in the Internet Era: Every cultural good from the past will be found, harvested and exhausted.

But that's not quite true. Most games are never resurrected. They offer nothing because they are, ultimately, nothing. Manifestations of the market that transform into perishable products. When enough people are interested in vampires and cyberpunks, you

---

37   Infectious bacteria + JGJ = fun?

get *Bloodnet*. Cash grabs as inevitable as the risen sun. You can beg it not to come up. But it always does.

John George Jones is different. No one asked for *Go to Hell*. No one wanted *Soft & Cuddly*. His games are works of art that have revealed themselves through time. Slogging through the years, their meaning shifting and changing with the era, somehow unsullied by money.

•

Thirty years ago, one person could make a game. Level-design, graphics, sound, mechanics, programming. By themselves, alone. In their mom's basement.

Not long after *Soft & Cuddly*'s release, this model would disappear. Games and systems became too complex for one individual.

Sure, some people slaved in obscurity on games that would never find audiences, but literally no one in the world believed that we'd move back to a model where the lone programmer could produce and commercially release a viable game.

And then came Steam.

After everything shifted, when development again resembled the old model, Earl C. gave birth to *Fucker Gamer Scum Get Stabbed*. He put the thing together in a week. On a computer 10,000 times as powerful as the ZX Spectrum.

Here, now, in our time.
Soft & Cuddly and *Go to Hell* live again.

BUT.
WHAT
THE
FUCK
WILL
THEY
MEAN
TOMORROW
?

NOTES

Sources consulted for multiple chapters:

- *Alice Cooper Goes to Hell* by Alice Cooper (Warner Bros., 1976)
- *In Plain Sight: The Life and Lies of Jimmy Savile* by Dan Davies (Quercus, 2014)
- *Sinclair and the Sunrise Technology: The Deconstruction of a Myth* by Ian Adamson and Richard Kennedy (Penguin, 1986)
- *The Sinclair Story* by Rodney Dale (Gerald Duckworth & Co., 1985)
- World of Spectrum (http://bit.ly/2f6a09M)
- Numerous computer games magazines hosted at the Internet Archive's Computer Magazine Archives (http://bit.ly/1gLvmpi)

Chapter 1

The following sources were consulted for this chapter:

- "Where's There's Yuk, There's Brass" by Mel Croucher in *The Games Machine* #2, December 1987, page 24.
- *Ban This Filth!: Letters from the Mary Whitehouse Archive* by Ben Thompson (Faber & Faber, 2012), specifically page 104 for the letter on Alice Cooper.
- "From Alice Cooper to Marilyn Manson: The Significance of Adolescent Antiheroes," *Academic Psychiatry* vol.27, no.1 (Spring 2003) by Jeff Q. Bostic, MD, Ed.D, Steve Scholzman, M.D., Caroly Pataki, M.D., Carel Ristuccia, Eugene V. Beresin, M.D., Andrés Martin, M.D., M.P.H.
- *KISS: Behind the Mask: The Official Authorized Biography* by David Leaf and Ken Sharp (Grand Central Publishing), page 180.
- "New Gory Shocker," *Star*, August 26, 1987.

And for the curious, "Geber hain götcu! Amına böyle koydum!" translates to "Die, treacherous assfucker! I put it in your cunt!"

Chapter 2

This chapter, in particular, is super-dependent on Dale's *The Sinclair Story* and Adamson & Kennedy's *Sinclair and the Sunrise Technology*.

Chapter 3

The following sources were consulted for this chapter:

- "Enter the Video Nasties," *ZZap!64* #2, June 1985, page 69.
- "New York Day by Day" by Clyde Haberman and Laurie Johnston, *New York Times*, October 15, 1982, for the fury over Custer's Revenge.
- "What's New in Video Games; The Brouhaha Over X-rated Games" by Andrew Pollack, *New York Times*, October 24, 1982.
- "Jim Levy and Activision" posted by Jimmy Maher on his blog The Digital Antiquarian November 5, 2014 (http://bit.ly/2fiFmHN)
- "Out of the Frying Pan…", another Digital Antiquarian post from December 12, 2014 (http://bit.ly/2fXD3dn)
- Activision's annual reports from 1985 through 1990 (the latter two years produced under Activision's short stint as MEDIAGENIC) are held on microfiche at Stanford University Libraries.

Chapter 4

John le Carré's *Tinker, Tailor, Soldier, Spy* was first released in 1974 in the UK by Hodder & Stoughton.

Philip Sandifer's essay "Pop Between Realities, Home in Time For Tea 23 (The Winter of Discontent)" is currently hosted at Eruditorum Press (http://bit.ly/2g0sbNe) and has been published in volume 5 of Tardis Eruditorum.

The following articles in *Popular Computing Weekly* trace the clusterfuck of the Spectrum's release:

- "Sinclair Strikes Back at the BBC," May 6, 1982, pages 10-11, 18.
- "Editorial," June 10, 1982, page 3.
- "Design Flaw halts Spectrum Delivery," June 17, 1982, page 5.
- "ZX82 back in full production," June 24, 1982, page 5.
- "Spectrum get to the customer," July 1, 1982 page 5.
- "Long wait still for the Spectrum," July 15, 1982, page 5.
- "Hey! Where's ma Spectrum," August 5, 1982, page 7.
- "Spectrum delay prompts gift offer," August 19, 1982 page 5.
- "Spectrum plugs in new sockets," October 7, 1982, page 5.
- "Spectrum goes on sale at W H Smith," December 16, 1982, page 5.

Margaret Thatcher's scheme to install computers into every primary school in Britain was covered by Peter Large's "Primaries Get £9m computer switch-on," *Guardian*, July 17, 1982, page 2.

"Gotcha! Our lads sink gunboat and hole cruiser" was the headline of the May 4, 1982 issue of the *Sun*.

A clip of Thatcher presenting Zenko Suzuki with a functioning ZX Spectrum can be seen here: https://youtu.be/KpuEIiAHG94

The full text of Thatcher's Dec 8, 1982 speech is hosted by the Margaret Thatcher Foundation: http://bit.ly/2gj8ROM

Chapter 5

The full text of Thatcher's speech to the Conservative Council is also hosted by the Margaret Thatcher Foundation: http://bit.ly/2f2fLBS

For information on Matt Smith, creator of *Manic Miner* and *Jet Set Willy*, the following sources were consulted:

- "Whatever Happened to the J.D. Salinger of Gaming?" by Mike Pattenden, *Guardian,* July 19, 2015.

- "Feature: The Gospel According To Matthew Smith" by Simon Carless, posted January 2, 2007 to GameSetWatch (http://bit.ly/2fYNf98)
- "Matthew Smith Interview Manic Miner ZX Spectrum" (https://youtu.be/FWmmMZlhcqU)
- "Where is Matthew Smith?" by Stephen Smith (http://bit.ly/2f2a4nJ)
- "Matthew Smith and Manic Miner on Thumb Candy" (https://youtu.be/-ngGU4tUDLM)

The 1984 episode of *Commercial Breaks* featuring Imagine Software, "The Battle for Santa's Software," is available at the Internet Archive (http://bit.ly/2f66gFo) and on YouTube (https://youtu.be/ChmQBK_EaUQ).

Chapter 6

Is there any point to citing the manual to *Go to Hell*?

Chapter 7

This chapter is almost entirely dependent on Adamson & Kennedy's *Sinclair and the Sunrise Technology*.

Chapter 8

The illustrations in this chapter were gathered from Bill Gilbert's "Full Tape Crack Pack" hosted at http://bit.ly/2f66tbx.

Chapter 9

Image and text for John George Jones's interview comes from "C.O.D.E. T.A.L.K.: John George Jones," *Sinclair User* #67, October 1987, page 37.

Chapter 10

H.E.X.'s "To Be and Iron Maiden" is available on YouTube here: https://youtu.be/CXVdTIkcgGQ

Chapter 11

Philip Snout barks and slavers over *Soft & Cuddly*'s instructions in "YS Tipshop," *Your Sinclair* #26, February 1988, page 38.

Chapter 13

The following sources were consulted for this chapter:

- "Soft & Cuddly," *Crash* # 44, September 1987, page 108.
- "X-Rated Software: Do You Dare Look at some of the horrors currently on sale?" *Sinclair User* #67, October 1987, page 31.

- "Lloyd Mangram's FORUM," *Crash* #46, November 1987, page 40 (both the letter and editorial response)
- *Can of Worms* cassette inlay, accessed from Simon Holdsworth's "ZX81 Tapes, Hardware and Books Collection" (http://bit.ly/2gj3MGm)
- "Where's There's Yuk, There's Brass," by Mel Croucher in *The Games Machine* #2, December 1987, pages 21-24,
- "The Messianic Approach to Computer Software or the Software Gospel According to Croucher…" *Crash* #27, April 1986, page 88.
- *Deus Ex Machina: The Best Game You Never Played in Your Life* by Mel Croucher (Acorn Books, 2014). Relevant information on his Dubai connections are available for inspection at Google Books: http://bit.ly/2fsDizA
- "Tell it to the Bear," *Sinclair User* #70, January 1988, page 44.

Epilogue

moroz1999's version of *Soft & Cuddly* is available for download at "VT Archiv": http://bit.ly/2fH4it7

Fucker Gamer Scum Get Stabbed is available for download here: http://bit.ly/2gj9x6X. Its creator, Earl C., may be contacted at chip@apedick.com.

ACKNOWLEDGEMENTS

FIRST AND FOREMOST: Josh Mast, who not only funded the publication of my novel *I Hate the Internet* but also turned me on to *Soft & Cuddly*. Some people shoot smack for fun. Josh ruins lives.

Second: A very special thanks must be extended to John George Jones, who submitted to a barrage of unsolicited emails and letters and very kindly met for tea in a downmarket Exeter café. There's nothing worse than an American who hunts you down and demands extended discussions about a bunch of shit that you did when you were a teenager and then tells you they're going to turn it all into a book. Despite this, JGJ was nothing but helpful and kind. I only hope he doesn't loathe the final product.

Third: Jason Scott, who's most responsible for Archive.org hosting scans of old gaming magazines. Without this resource, the book would have been impossible.

Fourth: Everyone who dealt with my entreaties. Sorry so little of your interviews made it into the book. I thought it would all add up to more than it did. Andy Wood, Wayne Allen, Rod Cousens CBE, Geoff Heath OBE, Peter Bilotta, Anthony Baring, Roger Large, Hugh Rees-Parnall, Allison Hale, Graeme Devine, Jacek Michalak, Andrew Wright, Ray Hodges, Earl C., Clem Chambers, and Ashley Hildebrandt. Thank you all for your patience regarding some crazy old bullshit.

Fifth: Jimmy Maher who runs The Digital Antiquarian on the inexplicably named filfre.net. The ultimate inspiration for writing about games. Update more frequently.

Sixth: The incomparable and incomprehensible Stanley Schtinter of purge.xxx. Thanks for the help, pal.

Finally: Boss Fight.

SPECIAL THANKS

For making our third season of books possible, Boss Fight Books would like to thank Maxwell Neely-Cohen, Cathy Durham, Edwin Locke, Mark Kuchler, Ken Durham, alraz, Adam B Wenzel, Sam Grawe, Jared Wadsworth, Sean Flannigan, Angus Fletcher, Patrick Tenney, Joshua Mallory, Brit W., Tomio Ueda, Joel Bergman, Sunjay Kelkar, Joe Murray, David Hayes, and Shawn Reed.

ALSO FROM
BOSS FIGHT BOOKS

1. *EarthBound* by Ken Baumann
2. *Chrono Trigger* by Michael P. Williams
3. *ZZT* by Anna Anthropy
4. *Galaga* by Michael Kimball
5. *Jagged Alliance 2* by Darius Kazemi
6. *Super Mario Bros. 2* by Jon Irwin

7. *Bible Adventures* by Gabe Durham
8. *Baldur's Gate II* by Matt Bell
9. *Metal Gear Solid* by Ashly & Anthony Burch
10. *Shadow of the Colossus* by Nick Suttner
11. *Spelunky* by Derek Yu
12. *World of Warcraft* by Daniel Lisi

13. *Super Mario Bros 3* by Alyse Knorr
14. *Mega Man 3* by Salvatore Pane
15. *Soft & Cuddly* by Jarett Kobek
16. *Kingdom Hearts II* by Alexa Ray Corriea
17. *Katamari Damacy* by L.E. Hall

★   *Continue? The Boss Fight Books Anthology*